S. Hrg. 113–201

SYRIA

HEARING

BEFORE THE

COMMITTEE ON FOREIGN RELATIONS UNITED STATES SENATE

ONE HUNDRED THIRTEENTH CONGRESS

FIRST SESSION

OCTOBER 31, 2013

Printed for the use of the Committee on Foreign Relations

Available via the World Wide Web: http://www.gpo.gov/fdsys/

U.S. GOVERNMENT PRINTING OFFICE

86–865 PDF   WASHINGTON : 2014

For sale by the Superintendent of Documents, U.S. Government Printing Office
Internet: bookstore.gpo.gov   Phone: toll free (866) 512–1800; DC area (202) 512–1800
Fax: (202) 512–2104   Mail: Stop IDCC, Washington, DC 20402–0001

COMMITTEE ON FOREIGN RELATIONS

ROBERT MENENDEZ, New Jersey, *Chairman*

BARBARA BOXER, California
BENJAMIN L. CARDIN, Maryland
JEANNE SHAHEEN, New Hampshire
CHRISTOPHER A. COONS, Delaware
RICHARD J. DURBIN, Illinois
TOM UDALL, New Mexico
CHRISTOPHER MURPHY, Connecticut
TIM KAINE, Virginia
EDWARD J. MARKEY, Massachusetts

BOB CORKER, Tennessee
JAMES E. RISCH, Idaho
MARCO RUBIO, Florida
RON JOHNSON, Wisconsin
JEFF FLAKE, Arizona
JOHN McCAIN, Arizona
JOHN BARRASSO, Wyoming
RAND PAUL, Kentucky

DANIEL E. O'BRIEN, *Staff Director*
LESTER E. MUNSON III, *Republican Staff Director*

(II)

CONTENTS

SYRIA

THURSDAY, OCTOBER 31, 2013

U.S. SENATE,
COMMITTEE ON FOREIGN RELATIONS,
Washington, DC.

The committee met, pursuant to notice, at 10:16 a.m., in room SD–419, Dirksen Senate Office Building, Hon. Robert Menendez (chairman of the committee) presiding.

Present: Senators Menendez, Cardin, Shaheen, Coons, Durbin, Udall, Murphy, Kaine, Markey, Corker, Risch, Rubio, Johnson, Flake, and McCain.

OPENING STATEMENT OF HON. ROBERT MENENDEZ, U.S. SENATOR FROM NEW JERSEY

The CHAIRMAN. This Senate Foreign Relations Committee will come to order. We have two panels today. Our first panel is: Robert Ford, Ambassador to Syria; Nancy Lindborg, who is the Assistant Administrator for the Bureau of Democracy, Conflict and Humanitarian Assistance at USAID; and Thomas Countryman, Assistant Secretary of State for International Security and Nonproliferation.

On our second panel we will have Ambassador Frederic Hof, a senior fellow at the Rafik Hariri Center for the Middle East on the Atlantic Council, and Dr. Leslie Gelb, the president emeritus of the Council on Foreign Relations. We welcome you all.

I look forward in this hearing to hearing your perspective on the realities we face in Syria, the state of play, the progress we have made, and where we go from here strategically, especially given the catastrophic humanitarian crisis that is spreading across the region. Seven million Syrians, a third of the country's population, have fled their homes. More than 2 million refugees, half of them children, have fled to surrounding countries.

The regional impact is enormous. In tiny Lebanon, for example, the presence of 750,000 refugees is equivalent to some 58 million refugees entering the United States.

Clearly, with 4,000 refugees fleeing Syria every day, for the sake of the region and the world we must find a resolution to this devastating humanitarian crisis. Now we read reports of a breakdown in Syria's health services, with the World Health Organization warning that confirmed cases of polio could just be the tip of the iceberg and a significant setback in the campaign to eradicate polio worldwide.

While responsible players in the international community seek to address the humanitarian crisis, there is no end in sight to the suffering. Despite the fact that most of us today would agree that a

(1)

negotiated settlement is certainly preferable to any military action or the collapse of the Syrian state, the utter lack of consensus on the transitional governance plan for Syria portends continued bloodshed and suffering.

While the international community holds meetings about meetings, the Assad regime continues its brutal assault on the Syrian people, backed by Iran, Russia, and Hezbollah. At this point, the consequences of failure to achieve a political settlement are frightening. A failed Syrian state bordering Iraq, Lebanon, Turkey, Jordan, and our ally Israel becomes a haven and training ground for violent extremist groups in an already unstable region.

So I am concerned about what comes next strategically at the political, diplomatic, and humanitarian levels. I would like to hear from each of you what our strategy should be going forward and your assessments of the direction of the conflict. Will the Geneva conference take place in November? How can it take place when the Syrian opposition remains fragmented and resistant? How can it take place without empowering Assad, and what are the consequences if there are no steps taken toward negotiations?

What needs to happen for the Syrian opposition to unite in political purpose in a post-Assad governance plan? Does the United States-recognized Syrian opposition speak for Syrians inside of Syria? And how can we galvanize international support for a negotiated settlement, especially when Assad is backed by those in Moscow and Teheran who see a different set of goals? What is the impact of the concerns raised by our gulf partners about United States commitment to addressing the Syrian crisis? And worst of all, what are the consequences of a failed state in Syria?

I do want to take note of some, I think very important progress that was, I think, largely fueled by the vote of this committee for the use of force, that allowed the President to make it clear what would be his intentions if there could not be a negotiation. That is the progress we are making on destroying and dismantling Syria's chemical weapons infrastructure and supply.

Today the Organization for the Prohibition of Chemical Weapons confirmed that it has destroyed the equipment Syria used to make chemical weapons, and so far inspectors have visited 21 of the 23 chemical sites initially identified by Syrian authorities within the timeframe that was specified, which would be tomorrow. The two remaining sites are in contested areas where the challenge of getting there is more difficult, but I hope ultimately can be succeeded at as well.

So let me begin by saying I want to make clear my views at the outset. The United States cannot, and should not, be the key that resolves every dispute in this region, but we have a very real strategic stake in the stability of the region and ensuring that Syria does not become a failed state. I believe we need to further increase our humanitarian assistance and insist on humanitarian access, as well as increase our support to communities hosting Syrian refugees in Lebanon and Jordan, and to getting others in the international community to live up to their responsibilities in this regard, calling on donor nations to join us in its time of greatest need, because Syria is now, from my perspective, a global problem.

Finally, we need an answer as to what we can do to push all sides in this conflict toward a settlement and a future for Syria that does not include Assad. The stakes are high for the people of Syria, for the region and the world, and we need to have a comprehensive strategy and an answer to the basic question, what comes next.

Senator Corker.

OPENING STATEMENT OF HON. BOB CORKER, U.S. SENATOR FROM TENNESSEE

Senator CORKER. Thank you, Mr. Chairman.

I want to thank the witnesses of both panels for being here today and I look forward to your testimony. I want to also thank the committee. I think—and your leadership, Mr. Chairman. We have had two, I think, really big steps that have taken place in this committee.

One was laying out a strategy for Syria that passed on a 15–3 vote in this committee. Regardless of how people voted, I think it was one of the finer moments of this committee.

Secondly, you remember, I think everybody remembers, Secretary Kerry came in on September 3 asking for the authorization for the use of military force, which was passed out of this committee at his request and at the President's request. At that time the Secretary said there was a strategy relative to Syria. As a matter of fact, it was a strategy similar to what was laid out in this committee.

Obviously, things have changed pretty dramatically on the ground since that time with the issue of the chemical weapons. Basically as far as I can see there is no real strategy relative to the opposition. I know that we are still verbalizing that there is a strategy. I look forward especially to Ambassador Ford's testimony regarding the opposition.

But let us face it, guys: What really happened when the Russian offer came forth was it was less about seizing an opportunity and it was more about our country not having the stomach to follow through on a strategy over the longer term relative to Syria. Now, look, I very much hope that we are successful and think we will be relative to chemical weapons. But in the process we have diminished our standing in the Middle East. I think everybody watching understands that in essence we've thrown out any real strategy there and are just trying to figure out a way out of this. We have empowered Assad. We have weakened ourselves relative to other issues in the Middle East.

So I am very disappointed. I do hope that somehow things that are good come out of this for our Nation. I want to support any and every diplomatic effort that is taking place. But I think we ought to realize there is no strategy right now for the opposition; none. There is no strategy.

For that reason, there is unlikely to be a very successful Geneva 2 conference, because who is it that we are going to be dealing with? Who is it that we are going to be bringing to the table? So I think we have, again, weakened ourselves. I hope there is a good outcome and I hope there are other opportunities for this committee to be involved in some good outcomes. But I do look forward to our witnesses today; their testimony. I look forward to them helping us help the administration and help our Nation develop a better longer term strategy in Syria.

Mr. Chairman, I thank you for calling this timely hearing.

The CHAIRMAN. Ambassador Ford, we will start with you.

STATEMENT OF HON. ROBERT S. FORD, U.S. AMBASSADOR TO SYRIA, U.S. DEPARTMENT OF STATE, WASHINGTON, DC

Ambassador FORD. Thank you, Mr. Chairman, Ranking Member Corker, and members of the committee. Thank you for the opportunity to come and give you an update on the United States Government's Syria policy. I have submitted written testimony for the record.

I have been alternating, one week in Washington and one week in the Middle East, for the last month as we have worked to provide assistance to the moderate opposition and as we push for a political settlement. Let me focus on those two elements, strategy with the opposition and focus on the political settlement, and I will let my colleagues, Assistant Secretary Countryman and Assistant Administrator Lindborg, talk about chemical weapons and humanitarian assistance issues.

The conflict in Syria now is a grinding war of attrition. The regime is suffering serious manpower shortages. For that reason, it has brought in foreign fighters from Hezbollah, from the Iran Revolutionary Guard Corps, and even Iraqi Shia militiamen. Meanwhile, the moderate opposition that we support is fighting on two fronts, both against the regime and against militants, extremists, directly linked to Al Qaeda in Iraq—the same Al Qaeda in Iraq that we used to fight.

The battle front in Syria is more complicated now, but neither the regime nor the various opposition factions can throw a knockout punch in the foreseeable future. Our strategy is based on that assessment. Secretary Kerry therefore is working extensively with Russia, with other concerned members of the international community, including countries like us that strongly support the Syrian opposition, and he is working with the United Nations to promote a political solution.

Last week on October 22 in London, 11 countries that strongly support the Syrian opposition came together and we all reaffirmed our support for a negotiated settlement based on the full implementation—I want to underline that, full implementation—of the June 2012 Geneva communique. This full implementation of the Geneva communique is also what we have agreed upon during the summer with the United Nations and the Russian Government.

We, the Russians, the London 11 countries, and the United Nations all agree that a Geneva peace conference should result in the creation of a transition governing body established by mutual agreement between the Syrian regime and the opposition. This is a political solution which most Syrians and those countries supporting the opposition and supporting the regime would back.

We have confirmed with the Russians during our summer discussions and among the 11 countries that just met in London that mutual consent—I mentioned mutual consent to set up this government—mutual consent would mean the opposition has a veto on the formation and the details of that transition government.

Speaking frankly, no one who knows the groups that are resisting and fighting the regime now thinks they will ever accept Assad. That said, the regime also has a veto. So if we do get to a Geneva conference we can expect very tough negotiations.

The Syrian opposition has a role to play here. It needs to tell other Syrians not only what it rejects, but also what it proposes in terms of a reasonable alternative to the existing Assad regime. It needs to put that on the table. Why? Because many of the people who support the regime now do so fearfully. I have heard this repeatedly from them, from people I have met. They want to know, is there a way out of the conflict? The Russians, who back the regime but say they are not tied to Assad, they too want to see the opposition put forward an alternative.

So the opposition has a lot of work to do in this regard. And that reasonable alternative is especially needed now because of the growing competition between extremists and moderates inside Syria. Mr. Chairman, members of the committee, I really want to emphasize that we have to weigh in on behalf of those who promote freedom and tolerance within the Syrian opposition, people who resist the regime, but who also resist al-Qaeda-linked extremists. I said that last spring when I appeared before you and it is even more true today.

Our nonlethal support of the moderate-armed opposition is therefore vital, and it is a point that General Idriss of the Supreme Military Council has made to me repeatedly. More broadly, since the start of the conflict we have provided over $250 million in nonlethal assistance to the coalition and a range of local councils, grassroots groups, to help preserve institutions of governance in places where the Syrian regime has withdrawn.

As I have told this committee before, Syria presents incredibly difficult challenges. We will continue working to support the moderates in the opposition and to push forward on a political solution. We look forward to working with the Congress as we move ahead.

Thank you again for the opportunity to come before you today and I will be happy to take questions.

Thank you.

[The prepared statement of Ambassador Ford follows:]

PREPARED STATEMENT OF AMBASSADOR ROBERT S. FORD

Chairman Menendez, Ranking Member Corker, and members of the committee, thank you for inviting me to present an overview of our policy to promote political transition in Syria.

This hearing is timely, due to recent developments. As I have also just returned from travel for meetings in Europe and the region, I can share with you the results of the Department's efforts to press the parties toward negotiations as well as working with our partners to bolster international support.

As we finalize and put into action a plan to end Syria's chemical weapons program and stockpile, which my colleague, Assistant Secretary Countryman, will address, we have doubled-down on our diplomatic efforts to bring the parties together to negotiate an end to the conflict. A negotiated political transition that rids Syria of Assad and his ruling clique, while preserving civil order, is the best means to stem the bloodshed as well as counter the growth of extremist groups taking advantage of the situation in Syria.

PREPARING FOR GENEVA

During my recent meetings with a host of opposition figures, all agreed that negotiations presented the best means to end the conflict. However, they also agreed that achieving a political transition that results in Assad's departure will not be easy. They fundamentally do not trust the Assad regime and are concerned that external parties will cut a deal at the opposition's expense.

These comments come from Syrian oppositionists who were thrown in prison, tortured by intelligence officials, and faced regular harassment and intimidation by both Bashar and his father, Hafez al-Asad. These are people who do not give up but are justifiably hesitant to sit down at a negotiating table across from representatives of a regime that has killed over tens of thousands of its own people, using chemical weapons, ballistic missiles, sniper bullets, aircraft, and heavy artillery.

Syria's opposition knows the Assad regime well; we cannot dismiss their views. During the October 22 meeting of the London 11 and in our communique from the meeting we have sought to bolster the opposition's confidence in approaching negotiations and assure them that, as the London 11 communique stipulates, "when a [transitional governing body] is established, Assad and his close associates with blood on their hands will have no role in Syria."

In the London 11 meeting, we also agreed that negotiations must not be open-ended and must result in implementation of the Geneva Communique principle of a transitional governing body exercising full executive powers, including over security and military forces in the country.

The London 11 agreed that the Syrian opposition will be represented by a single delegation headed by the Syrian Opposition Coalition (SOC) that will include other opposition representatives outside the coalition. This delegation must be representative if it is to assure Syria's many minority communities that Syria's future will be inclusive.

Since December 2012, the United States, along with our international partners, has recognized the SOC as the legitimate representative of the Syrian people. Comprised of diverse representatives inside and outside Syria, the coalition is committed to a democratic, inclusive Syria free from the influence of violent extremists.

The SOC has begun planning and preparation for negotiations. Although the SOC's leadership, including President Ahmed Issa al-Jarba support negotiating with the Syrian Government, they are deferring a decision to the General Assembly. While the outcome of a General Assembly vote, expected early in November, remains uncertain, the process of discussion within the General Assembly is useful in building a consensus and attaining a unified position.

SOC deliberations are not something for the U.S. to manage. It is an effort led by Syrians for Syrians that will define their desired outcomes. The SOC delegation will need genuine internal support to withstand Syrian regime negotiating tactics during the tough days ahead.

We have committed to building a process for the Syrian people to resolve the crisis themselves. The international community cannot do it for them. However, the international community and the United States in particular can support the Syrian opposition as they take the risky step forward in meeting with the other side.

U.S. ASSISTANCE

The conflict in Syria has fostered an environment that fuels the growth of extremism, and al-Qaeda-linked groups are working to exploit the situation for their own benefit. There is a real competition now between extremists and moderates in Syria and we need to weigh in on behalf of those who promote freedom and tolerance.

Since the start of the conflict, we have provided over $255 million in nonlethal assistance to the coalition and a range of local councils and grassroots groups inside Syria to build a network of ethnically and religiously diverse civilian activists from the top down as well as the bottom up. These funds are strengthening local councils, civil society groups, unarmed political activists, and free media to improve governance, accountability, and service delivery at the subnational and national level.

Our Liberated Areas Initiative is providing $10 million worth of generators, cranes, trucks, ambulances, and water bladders to areas under opposition control. During Ramadan, the United States provided 51,000 food baskets to a number of target areas in liberated areas mainly in northern Syria. Specifically, we have also provided 10 ambulances, 37 generators, 220 water storage units, and 5 firetrucks for local councils.

We boosted nine independent radio station signals, extending the reach of broadcast on FM stations, and funded three independent television stations. Those media platforms were used to address sectarian violence and issue public service messages on best practices in the event of chemical weapons exposure.

The United States has also trained over 15 local councils and civil society organizations to improve their responsiveness to community needs and their capacity to improve governance in the communities they support. About 61 local councils, 16 professional organizations, 42 media centers, and 106 civil society organizations have been represented at training funded by the U.S. Government for a total of nearly 3,000 activists trained.

Fierce fighting in Syria continues. Now with the regime dismantling its chemical weapons, it has returned to barbaric siege tactics on civilian areas that refuse to surrender.

In neighborhoods just minutes from Assad's gilded palace, children are dying while his forces are reportedly limiting access so severely that we are hearing the first reports of acute malnutrition as food aid and other assistance is blocked.

In the neighborhood of Muadhamiyyah, where the regime was so desperate to regain the upper hand that it used chemical weapons on August 21, it has allowed only a few thousand civilians to leave to provide cover for its attempts to choke off any supplies to the area for the remaining civilians.

The Syrian Government has ignored the demands by the U.N. Security Council, international humanitarian organizations, prominent religious leaders, and even its supporter, Russia, to allow the flow of humanitarian aid to these affected communities.

The best way for the regime to demonstrate it cares about the people of Syria and is ready to commit to work toward a resolution of this conflict is for it to allow assistance to flow to its own people.

SUPPORT TO THE ARMED OPPOSITION

There is no military solution to the conflict in Syria. Neither the regime nor the opposition has the wherewithal to militarily defeat the other. However, our support to the armed opposition is essential to our ability to maintain influence and to strengthen the position of moderates.

Our support assists Idriss and the SMC in their fight with extremist groups, who have targeted the moderate opposition. The Islamic State in Iraq and the Levant, an outgrowth of Al Qaeda in Iraq, has increasingly chosen to fight the moderate opposition. By empowering the moderates, we help them contest against extremists and terrorists.

Our nonlethal support of the moderate-armed opposition is important in keeping pressure on the regime. We greatly appreciate Congress' support, as we seek to provide the Supreme Military Council (SMC), led by General Salim Idriss, with 80 million dollars' worth of critical force enablers like vehicles, food, medical kits, and basic communications equipment.

To mitigate the risk that our assistance might end up in the hands of extremists, we will continue to rely on the effective, formal processes that have been established across various agencies in the government to vet the recipients of U.S. assistance.

CONCLUSION

The regime bears the responsibility for pursuing conflict rather than reform. The current situation was not inevitable. It sprang from a ruling clique that was willing to sacrifice its people to hold onto power. Assad has lost all legitimacy and must go. The regime and its backers have a choice—hold to the current approach and become a failing state beholden to foreign backers or take the higher road and shape the future of the country through negotiations.

Syrians are approaching the first opportunity to end over 2 years of civil war by starting negotiations. They do so in an atmosphere of distrust and apprehension. However, negotiations present the best chance for Syrians to define for themselves a vision of what freedom means in a new Syria. A future Syria must be inclusive of all its citizens in order to heal the wounds this civil war has inflicted.

A new, peaceful future for Syria is possible. It can be done. Negotiations will be a first step. We must, however, be realistic. Negotiations are unlikely to end quickly or be definitive on all points, including a constitution and new elections.

We support an inclusive, democratic transition. We continue to believe that is the best solution to the Syrian crisis. We also know that the opposition and the regime will need support to get to an agreement.

We look forward to working with Congress throughout this process. Thank you again for the invitation to testify before your committee today. I am happy to take your questions.

The CHAIRMAN. Secretary Countryman.

And all of your statements will be fully included in the record without objection.

STATEMENT OF HON. THOMAS M. COUNTRYMAN, ASSISTANT SECRETARY OF STATE FOR INTERNATIONAL SECURITY AND NONPROLIFERATION, U.S. DEPARTMENT OF STATE, WASHINGTON, DC

Mr. COUNTRYMAN. I want to thank you, Mr. Chairman, and thank the ranking member, Senator Corker, for this opportunity for a review of the progress made in the elimination of Syria's chemical weapons program. Today was the date that the Organization for the Prohibition of Chemical Weapons was able to announce that it had met the first target date in the program, completing the destruction of production, mixing, and filling equipment. I agree with both of you that the action of this committee last month contributed notably to the results we have achieved so far.

Since you have my written testimony, I would like to make just three quick points. First, our timetable. Our target dates are ambitious, but they are achievable. We have the support of the international community, including partners who are prepared to contribute financially and in terms of technology to achieving this goal. We have a very determined cadre of Federal employees in both the Defense Department, the State Department, and other agencies who are working hard to make sure that we have thought through a plan that is complicated but achievable in terms of logistics and security.

I am increasingly confident that we will be able to complete this task, the elimination of Syria's CW program, within the target date of June 30 of next year.

A couple of key factors that will contribute to the achievement of that target date and that, so far, are going well.

First, we discussed back in Geneva with the Russians that the removal of dangerous precursor chemicals from Syria, the bulk of which are not weaponized, not inside shells or warheads, would be essential to completing this task on time. The destruction plan submitted by the Syrian Government to the OPCW embraces exactly that concept and we are confident that we will have a host country that can work with us to effect the destruction outside of Syria of these precursor chemicals.

Secondly, our cooperation with the Russian Federation has so far been strong. We will continue to expect the Russian Government to press the Syrian Government for full compliance with its obligations. This will be essential as we move ahead.

Third, we continue this process with our eyes wide open. We are about to enter what could be the most complicated phase in terms of both logistics and security; that is the removal of chemical precursors in large quantities from several sites within Syria to the coast for removal on a ship to another country. That has both big logistical problems to think through and certain security risks.

At the same time, while the record so far is acceptable, we do not assume or take for granted that the Syrian Government will continue full compliance with its obligations. We have the tools we need, granted by the OPCW executive committee and by the United Nations Security Council, to press ahead on this goal. We intend to do so. This is why our statement, here and publicly, reflects the cautious optimism that we have at this point.

Thank you and I look forward to your questions.

[The prepared statement of Mr. Countryman follows:]

PREPARED STATEMENT OF HON. THOMAS M. COUNTRYMAN

Chairman Menendez, Ranking Member Corker, and members of the committee, thank you for inviting me to talk to you today about the efforts by the United Nations (U.N.) and the Organisation for the Prohibition of Chemical Weapons (OPCW) to complete and verify the elimination of the Syrian chemical weapons program. We have made significant progress in the month and a half that has passed since the negotiation of the U.S.-Russia Framework in Geneva (Framework). Considerable work remains to ensure the Syrian regime can never again use these weapons against its own people.

Two months ago, the Assad regime did not even publicly acknowledge that it possessed chemical weapons, despite having just perpetrated the worst chemical weapons attack in this century. As of today, OPCW inspectors on the ground in Syria, with U.N. support, have conducted inspections of 21 chemical weapons-related sites and verified the destruction of the production, mixing, and filling equipment at those sites. The OPCW has indicated that the Syrian Government is on target to complete the destruction of its chemical weapons production, and mixing/filling capabilities by November 1. The international community has come together to establish a firm legal framework, through U.N. Security Council Resolution (UNSCR) 2118 and a related decision by the OPCW Executive Council, to ensure that this immense undertaking is fulfilled in a transparent, expeditious, and verifiable manner—and within the ambitious but realistic timeline envisioned in the Framework. On September 14, the Syrian Government formally acceded to the Chemical Weapons Convention (CWC) and, in accordance with the CWC, UNSCR 2118, and an OPCW Executive Council decision, submitted a declaration of its CW materials and facilities to the OCPW on October 24, 2013.

The implementation of the Framework could not have been achieved absent the serious consideration of the use of force by the United States. It remains critically important, as this process continues, that members of the international community continue to monitor closely the Syrian regime's compliance with its CW-related obligations. Syria's obligations are quite clear, and we will continue to encourage Russia to advise the Assad regime about the wisdom of continued cooperation. The Security Council has already decided that, in the event of noncompliance with UNSCR 2118, it would impose chapter VII measures.

Last week, in conjunction with its initial declaration required by the CWC, the Syrian Government also submitted its required destruction plan to the OPCW. That plan was informed by technical-level conversations among U.S. and Russian experts and the OPCW Technical Secretariat in The Hague. While the CWC and OPCW require preserving confidentiality, I can say in this setting that the United States and Russia believe the destruction plan to be feasible and to conform to the terms outlined in the Framework. The plan also reflects our shared view that the removal and destruction of CW agent and precursor chemicals outside Syria, under OPCW verification, will be the most effective way to eliminate the vast majority of Syria's chemical weapons in the shortest possible time. With this in mind, UNSCR 2118 authorizes U.N. member states to acquire, control, transport, transfer, and destroy Syrian chemical weapons identified by the OPCW.

The task before us remains considerable and the timelines ambitious; ongoing Syrian cooperation with the U.N.–OPCW Joint Mission remains the key factor in successfully eliminating these weapons by mid-2014, as envisioned by the U.S.-Russia Framework. We expect the Russian Federation to continue to press Damascus to comply with these obligations and to permit the U.N.–OPCW Joint Mission to complete its work. With the continuing cooperation of the Syrian Government, the support of the international community, and the dedicated members of the U.N.–OPCW Joint Mission, we believe that this timeline is achievable. We have, of course, also been in close and continuous contact with Syrian opposition leaders, updating them throughout this process, and reiterating our expectation that they support and facilitate the activities of the U.N.–OPCW Joint Mission.

Let me say a word about the role of the United States and the international community in providing support to the U.N.–OPCW Joint Mission in Syria. We continue to encourage all countries to make whatever contribution they can to this important undertaking—whether that contribution is financial, technical, or in-kind—to enable the OPCW and U.N. to complete their missions. The United States has led by example in providing such support. U.S. assistance to the U.N. and OPCW already totals approximately $6 million from the State Department's Nonproliferation and Disarmament Fund, including direct financial assistance to both the U.N. and OPCW Trust Funds, as well as in-kind support for the inspection team. For example, as Secretary Kerry reported last week in London, the United States delivered 10 armored vehicles to support the efforts of the OPCW–U.N. Joint Mission in Syria.

We continue to approach this process with our eyes wide open. We can expect that the path ahead will not be smooth, given the unprecedented scope and timelines for the mission. But the positive developments in the 6 weeks since we left Geneva confirm that its timely completion is achievable. We are resolute in addressing these challenges given what is at stake for the Syrian people, the region, and the world.

Thank you again for the opportunity to discuss this important security issue with you. I look forward to your questions and to continuing to consult with you closely in the days ahead.

The CHAIRMAN. Thank you.
Administrator Lindborg.

STATEMENT OF HON. NANCY E. LINDBORG, ASSISTANT ADMINISTRATOR FOR THE BUREAU OF DEMOCRACY, CONFLICT AND HUMANITARIAN ASSISTANCE, UNITED STATES AGENCY FOR INTERNATIONAL DEVELOPMENT, WASHINGTON, DC

Ms. LINDBORG. Chairman Menendez, Ranking Member Corker, and members of the committee, thank you for inviting me to testify today and most especially thank you for your ongoing concern and for your support for humanitarian programs around the world. They are making a difference in the lives of many.

Since I last testified on this issue in front of this committee 7 months ago, there have been 30,000 additional deaths among the Syrians. In the last year the number of deaths has tripled to more than 100,000 and the number in need inside Syria has climbed to more than 6.8 million. This is equivalent to the total population of Vermont, New Hampshire, Maine, and Connecticut combined.

The pace of escalation is staggering. According to a recent U.N. report, in the 2 years of conflict Syria has lost 35 years of human development progress. With the 2 million refugees, this is a national crisis that has become a regional crisis, putting serious strains on the neighboring countries. Behind these jarring statistics is the real toll on the Syrian people—the kids who have not gone to school for 2 years; the women who have endured rape and abuse; and the 5 million internally displaced Syrians who do not have a place to live or enough to eat.

As the crisis has escalated, we have accelerated our humanitarian response. Our assistance is now reaching about 4.2 million people inside Syria and we are helping to support 2 million refugees. But the same stubborn challenges that I talked about 7 months ago—access, security, and resources—continue to prevent us and others from reaching everybody who needs help to get it, and the needs continue to escalate.

In early October, fueled by the political momentum of the Security Council's resolution to eliminate the chemical weapons, the U.N. Security Council unanimously passed a Presidential statement on humanitarian access. This statement urges all parties to the conflict to facilitate immediate access to all those affected, including going across borders and across conflict lines. This agreement represents the first and the most significant show of global political will to help those who need it most. The challenge now is to translate that commitment into real action on the ground.

Recent reports of starvation campaigns by the regime, of serious food shortages and disease outbreaks in areas that are literally blockaded, under siege by the regime, underscore the urgency.

The U.S. Government is working to mobilize the international community to act with the same intensity as it did around chemical weapons to ensure lifesaving assistance reaches those who need it desperately. In the meantime, we are continuing to provide humanitarian assistance through all possible channels, through the United Nations, through our NGO partners, through local Syrian organizations. Since this time last year, USAID has doubled the number of our partners working inside Syria and we have shored up systems and supply lines so that we can reach all 14 governates.

USAID is focused on four key areas, as detailed in my written testimony. In medical care, we have set up hundreds of medical facilities and treated hundreds of thousands of patients. We are working with an unbelievably courageous group of Syrian doctors and health workers who put their lives on the risk, lives at risk, on the front lines every day.

We are particularly concerned about the 10 cases of polio confirmed by WHO and are calling on all parties to allow access to the vaccination campaign that WHO now has under way.

Secondly, we remain the second-largest donor of emergency food. Our partners are now reaching more than 3 million people in Syria and a million refugees each month with food.

Third, a very tough winter is ahead. There are millions more displaced this year. So we are mobilizing a major winterization response.

As always, we are focused on protecting the most vulnerable. Women and children always fare the worst in the war. The Syria crisis is no exception. So we have elevated our focus on the scourge of gender-based violence and worked to provide assistance both inside and in the camps.

The single greatest factor limiting assistance remains the ongoing and intensifying conflict. The United Nations estimates that 2.5 million people in need have not received help in almost a year, and the regime is actively blockading whole communities. This is unconscionable and the recently passed U.N. agreement lays down very clear markers for the Syrian regime regarding the world's expectations that it will enable long-denied humanitarian access. We are encouraged that Russia and China supported this agreement and we must now see that support translated into meaningful pressure.

A quick word on the neighboring countries. We are working to combine our development and humanitarian resources so that we are providing help not just for the refugees, but for the host communities that are buckling under the strain of this influx of refugees. We are working closely with the international humanitarian donor community to make those resources count for the most.

In conclusion, humanitarian assistance will absolutely not end the bloodshed in Syria, but it is saving countless lives and it is alleviating very real pressures in the region. Your support has been absolutely vital.

So once again, thank you very much, and I look forward to questions.

[The prepared statement of Ms. Lindborg follows:]

PREPARED STATEMENT OF HON. NANCY E. LINDBORG

Chairman Menendez, Ranking Member Corker, and members of the committee; thank you for inviting me to testify on the ongoing U.S. response to Syria's humanitarian crisis. Thank you also for your continued support for our humanitarian programs around the world, which make a positive difference every day in the lives of millions.

INTRODUCTION

I last testified on the Syria crisis for the Senate Foreign Relations Subcommittee on Near Eastern and South and Central Asian Affairs 7 months ago and since then we have seen another 30,000 deaths, reflecting the staggering escalation of violence. In just the last year, the number of reported deaths has tripled from 26,000 to more than 100,000. The number in need inside Syria jumped from 2.5 million people to more than 6.8 million—roughly the equivalent of the combined populations of Vermont, New Hampshire, Maine, and Connecticut. And now with over 2 million refugees, a national crisis has fully evolved into a regional crisis, putting severe strains on vulnerable communities of neighboring countries.

According to a recent report released by the U.N., Syria has lost 35 years in human development as a result of 2½ years of this brutal conflict. And behind these jarring statistics is the very real toll on the people of Syria who survive—the women who continue to endure rape and violence; the "lost generation" of Syrian children now out of school for 2 years; and the roughly 5 million people displaced inside Syria with neither enough to eat nor a safe way out.

As the crisis has escalated, the United States has accelerated our humanitarian response at every step. We have now contributed nearly $1.4 billion in humanitarian assistance to help meet the urgent needs of 4.2 million people across all 14 governorates inside Syria and the more than 2 million refugees.

But the stubborn challenges of access, insecurity, and resources continue to prevent the international community from reaching all those who desperately need our help. Seized with the urgency of this crisis, in early October, and in the wake of concerted international action on securing chemical weapons, the U.N. Security Council unanimously adopted a Presidential Statement (PRST) on humanitarian access, urging all parties to the conflict to facilitate immediate humanitarian access to all those in need, importantly, across borders and conflict lines. To date, the PRST represents the first and most significant show of global political will to ensure humanitarian assistance reaches those who need it most. But now, we need this statement to translate into real action—and compliance—on the ground.

The urgency of real action is underscored by recent reports of serious food shortages and disease outbreaks among communities literally blockaded and made unreachable by the regime. And, as cold weather approaches, we anticipate increased reports of catastrophic needs. Coming on the heels of the U.N. Security Council resolution on the elimination of Syria's chemical weapons program, the U.S. Government is working with intensity to mobilize the international community to translate agreement into action on the ground to enable life-saving assistance to reach those Syrians desperately in need after 2 years of a brutal civil war.

Today, I'd like to update you on the U.S. Government humanitarian response and the challenges we still face.

THE U.S. HUMANITARIAN RESPONSE

The United States continues to work through all possible channels—the United Nations, international and nongovernmental organizations (NGOs), and local Syrian organizations—to reach those in need with life-saving supplies and services. Since this time last year, we have scaled up the number of our partners inside Syria from 12 to 26. To cope with a conflict with shifting lines, we have shored up systems and supply lines to increase our ability to reach all 14 governorates throughout the country.

U.S. humanitarian assistance in Syria is focused on four key areas: emergency medical care, food assistance, the provision of much-needed relief supplies, and the protection of vulnerable populations.

MEDICAL CARE

For almost 2 years, the U.S. Government has provided emergency medical care to those caught in the crossfire. Today, we support 260 medical facilities across Syria. These field hospitals and makeshift clinics have treated more than 940,000 patients and performed more than 113,000 surgeries. We have trained over 1,500 Syrian volunteers to provide emergency first aid care.

With the onset of warmer weather and communicable diseases on the rise last spring, we worked with partners to establish an early warning system for communicable diseases, which require early detection and fast response to prevent devastating consequences. We note with great concern the 10 cases of polio affecting underimmunized children under 2 in Syria's Dayr az Zawr Governorate that have been confirmed by the World Health Organization (WHO). WHO reports that immunizations have started in the area, but we remain concerned about the spread of this crippling and potentially deadly infectious disease.

The United States has also provided mental health support—such as operating child-friendly spaces, conducting emergency psychosocial first aid, and trainings in child protection—for more than 26,000 vulnerable people in internally displaced persons (IDP) camps and host communities. None of this vital medical assistance would be possible without the courage of the Syrian health workers who risk their lives on the front lines every day.

FOOD ASSISTANCE

The United States remains the single largest donor of emergency food assistance for the Syria crisis. Our partners, the U.N. World Food Programme (WFP) and nongovernmental organizations, now reach more than 3 million people inside Syria and over 1 million Syrian refugees in Jordan, Lebanon, Turkey, Iraq, and Egypt each month—and U.S. food aid presently accounts for more than one-third of all food assistance received by conflict-affected Syrian families.

USAID's Emergency Food Security Program enables us to deliver food assistance rapidly through a variety of flexible mechanisms—including local and regional purchase and voucher programs—that allow us to address food needs of Syrian refugees and invest in neighboring communities. Staying flexible is a central part of our approach and, without question, adds to our ability to help meet daily needs. Since January, for example, through partnerships with NGOs, we have supported delivery of approximately 18,000 metric tons of food to conflict-affected families in Aleppo governorate not reached by WFP, feeding over a quarter of a million people on a daily basis.

RELIEF SUPPLIES

With millions more displaced this winter than last, fierce winter forecasts, and heightened vulnerability after another year of conflict, the United States is focused on mobilizing a significant winterization response. In addition to basic supplies—communal cooking kits, blankets, mattresses, clothing, plastic sheeting, hygiene kits, water jugs—we are also improving infrastructure and shelters in camp and noncamp areas.

PROTECTION

All our humanitarian assistance programs seek to reach the most vulnerable populations—women, children, persons with disabilities, the elderly—who often face extraordinary levels of violence and abuse. Sadly, women and children often fare the worst in war, and the crisis in Syria is no exception. Gender-based violence (GBV) is a serious concern. U.S. Government medical support includes services for GBV survivors through women's health centers, mobile clinics, and outreach teams that provide health and psychosocial services to women who desperately need it. Simple solutions, like supporting all-purpose women's washing and gathering spaces in camps for the internally displaced, can prove life-changing.

Building on the momentum of the U.S. National Action Plan on Women, Peace, and Security as well as the U.S. Strategy to Prevent and Respond to Gender Based Violence Globally, Secretary Kerry announced a new $10 million global initiative last month in New York, called Safe from the Start—a joint Bureau for Population, Refugees, and Migration/USAID commitment to elevate our focus on the scourge of GBV. In Syria, that means we have looked at all of our programs with the goal of prioritizing and incorporating protection for women and children.

KEY CHALLENGES

But the single-greatest factor limiting humanitarian aid remains the ongoing, intensifying conflict. Despite persistent pushing for greater humanitarian access, including across borders, the U.N. still estimates that 2.5 million people in need have not received help for almost a year. The regime continues to actively blockade whole communities.

This siege on civilians is unconscionable. The recently passed PRST lays down markers for the Syrian regime regarding the world's expectations that it will provide international humanitarian relief agencies with the immediate and unfettered access they have long been denied. It outlines very specific steps that are essential to facilitate the expansion of humanitarian relief operations and address the obstacles that already exist on the ground. These steps include:

- Immediately demilitarizing medical facilities, schools, and water stations and refraining from targeting all civilian objects;
- Approving access for additional domestic and international NGOs;
- Easing and expediting the operationalization of humanitarian hubs, the entry and movement of humanitarian personnel and convoys by granting necessary visas and permits;
- Accelerating the importation of humanitarian goods and equipment like communications tools, protective armored vehicles, and medical and surgical equipment; and, most importantly,
- Facilitating humanitarian workers' immediate and unfettered access to people in need.

There are concrete steps that the Syrian regime can take to allow the international community to reach innocent civilians caught in the crossfire. For example, we have seen some instances of aid delivery across battle lines so we know such access is possible. Through delicate negotiations with the Syrian Government and opposition factions, and with the critical partnership of the Syrian Coalition, approximately 30 U.N.-sponsored convoys reached displaced Syrians through cross-line efforts from January to September 2013. But more help is urgently needed, and time is not on our side.

The U.S. Government is seized with this issue, but getting the Syrian regime to comply will require coordinated diplomatic support from all sides. We were encouraged by Russia and China's support for the PRST and now, this support must be followed with significant pressure. U.S. diplomats are working with key international actors that have influence in Syria to convince all parties to the conflict to expand humanitarian access now.

ASSISTANCE TO NEIGHBORING COUNTRIES AND HOST COMMUNITIES

With more than 2 million Syrian refugees in neighboring countries, this crisis is now truly regional, threatening the stability of nations struggling to support this massive influx. As these countries host growing refugee communities, our commitment is to continue to support both refugees and those host communities bearing much of the brunt.

Beyond food, medical care, and other traditional relief supplies, U.S. Government assistance for refugees includes innovative methods to meet the needs of refugees living in urban populations, such as food vouchers and debit cards for use in local markets, and cash assistance to help refugees pay rent. On my last visit to the region in August, I met with Syrian refugees now living in the outskirts of Amman, who named the cost of rent as their greatest concern.

With the majority of Syrian refugees now living outside camps, U.S. Government support for food vouchers and other emergency food assistance to Syrian refugees now totals more than $177 million, injecting cash into local economies and alleviating pressures on communities that are hosting refugees.

U.S. assistance for host communities was a major focus of my travel in August to Jordan and Lebanon, where in some cases Syrian refugees now outnumber the Jordanian or Lebanese people in villages, and vital resources like water are already scarce. In both countries, we see that the poorest communities clearly overlap with the greatest concentration of refugees. Tensions between locals and refugees over resources exist in both countries, so we are paying close attention to key infrastructure, health, and education programming and ramping up efforts to help ensure delivery of essential services at the local level so host communities directly benefit from our assistance.

In Jordan, where domestic water supply is among the lowest in the world, USAID's Complex Crises Fund (CCF) not only helps communities withstanding mass influxes of refugees to access clean water themselves but also to improve water use efficiency, meaning they can provide water for their livestock and sustain their livelihoods. More recently, we launched a $21 million Community Engagement Project that works closely with communities to identify their most pressing challenges and meet growing community needs: school infrastructure, public parks preservation, lighting, medical equipment, and youth clubs. These programs are helping the Jordanian people and their communities cope with the influx and continue to welcome the influx and continue to welcome Syrian refugees.

In Lebanon, where an estimated one quarter of the population is now Syrian refugees and the spillover effects of the crisis appear the most acute, we are similarly focused on water and education as well as a value-chain development program to advance agriculture in heavily affected areas like the Bekaa Valley in Lebanon's northeast.

Providing support to host communities will be an ongoing challenge for the international community. We are partnering with host country governments and the international donor community to prioritize development assistance needs, including in Jordan where the Government of Jordan, along with UNHCR and UNDP, is developing a Host Community Coordination Platform to coordinate direct humanitarian and development support to host communities. At the request of the Government of Lebanon, the World Bank recently released a "Roadmap" identifying priority assistance areas to help Lebanon manage the impact of the Syrian crisis and develop the public service infrastructure needed to sustain the dramatic increases in its population.

These partnerships and assessments are vital to charting an effective way forward as we work to address the long-term effects of Syria's protracted conflict. Well aware that Syria's humanitarian crisis now presents a fundamental development challenge for the region, international humanitarian and development donors will reconvene in Amman next week to continue mapping coordinated efforts essential to alleviating immediate pressures on neighboring populations—and ensuring the stability and long-term development of countries in the region.

CONCLUSION

Humanitarian assistance will not end the bloodshed in Syria, but it is saving lives and helping alleviate the very real pressures this protracted conflict has put on the lives of everyday people throughout the region. The United States remains fully committed to a strong humanitarian response—and to coordinating closely with our international development partners—to help the Syrian people and Syria's neighbors endure this crisis. Your congressional support has been vital in enabling lifesaving humanitarian assistance work throughout the region.

The breakthrough agreement among members of the United Nations Security Council on the elimination of Syria's chemical weapons program, followed closely by the issuance of a statement endorsing emergency assistance to Syrians, has given new hope to aid workers inside Syria. These aid workers, most of them Syrian, have risked their lives daily to ensure help reaches those most in need, but effective humanitarian action will require cooperation from the Assad regime, opposition groups, and the foreign governments that until now have allowed their Syrian allies to stand in the way of or undermine relief operations.

Thank you for your time, and I look forward to your questions.

The CHAIRMAN. Thank you all for your testimony.

We will start a round of questions here. Let me say, Ambassador Ford, I heard your statement and I appreciate your incredible service, but I did not hear a strategy. That to me is challenging at this date.

Now, I understand that in Syria there are not great options. This is a pretty bad hand that the region, as well as all of us who care about it, have been dealt. But in the midst of that there has to be some effort of a strategy to get us to where we need to be. Assad is saying he will attend Geneva if there are no preconditions. That is a redline for the opposition. The opposition, as you stated is fragmented, has its own work to do to offer a vision of where they will come.

Assad's talking about running for President in 2014. He sees himself as an indispensable partner as it relates to the elimination of the chemical weapons program. And the Russians, in a war that you described in which there is no one to deliver a knockout punch, will continue to stand by Assad.

So in the face of all of that, what is our strategy? What is our strategy to get the Russians? What do we need to determine with the Russians what it will take for them to change their calculus? What is our strategy to get the moderate, vetted elements of the opposition to be able to come together with a plan for the country?

What is our strategy to be able to get the Russians to help us, assuming that can be done, to press Assad to ultimately leave? What is our strategy to continue to move forward on the chemical weapons destruction, as we are trying to do all these things together?

I just do not get a sense that we have a strategy. I wish that the authorization that this committee passed back in May would have been used at that time, because the dynamics were different and I think we could have far better effected the efforts toward the negotiation that we still aspire to. But the administration chose not to use that at the time.

So give me a sense of what this strategy is, because I did not glean it from your remarks?

Ambassador FORD. Senator, it is a two-track strategy. It is a two-track strategy. First, keep pushing to get the two sides to the table. But we understand that the Assad regime is a very tough, brutal regime. Nancy went through some of the details; the suffering inflicted on the Syrian people. So we will have to have pressure on the regime to get them to make concessions at the table.

Now, the pressure can come from a couple of places. One, it will come on the ground. So we have—we the Americans—organized a group of 11 countries, which I referred to, who are the primary backers of both the political and the armed opposition, and we coordinate our efforts on that. We call that group the London 11. It includes the Gulf States, it includes European states. The main backers of the Syrian opposition meet regularly, both at my level and at the Secretaries level, most recently, as I said, October 22.

So push for negotiations, but help the moderate opposition be in a position itself to press for concessions from the regime when it gets there.

Now, the other source of pressure will be the Russians. Secretary Kerry has talked extensively with Russian Foreign Minister Lavrov. They speak regularly, several times a week, on Syria. The Russians share a big interest with us in Syria about not having that country, as it becomes a failed state, become a base of extremism. They have their own national security interests in that respect.

They are concerned about the country, were Assad to leave, becoming a totally anarchical place, and they therefore talk about the need for a managed transition. But you cannot have a managed transition until the opposition itself puts forward proposals that the Russians and others can look at, Senator. Otherwise, we are in a sort of an absurd chicken and egg situation.

So I have been talking extensively to the opposition about putting some things on the table that the Russians and the rest of the international community and, most importantly, other Syrians can look at to say there is an alternative.

The CHAIRMAN. Can you give us a sense of what that would be, that would assuage both the Syrian people and the Russians to unite behind the opposition?

Ambassador FORD. For example, if Assad were to go, Senator, who would replace him as President and what would his authorities be? We have talked to the Russians extensively about what that would be and we have agreed with them that the new transition governing body will have full authority over the intelligence establishment, over the military establishment, over the financial structure of the country and the government. So we have agreed on that with the Russians.

But now we need the opposition to come forward and say: This is how we would put it together. Very frankly, Senator, they were so busy pushing us to intervene militarily that they have left aside the need to put forward this alternative, which sooner or later must come. Sooner or later it must come.

So were they to put that forward now, the Russians would at least have an opportunity to study it. I do not think they would accept it at face value. But it is something where you can begin a process. That is our strategy, to get a process started where all of us, moderate opposition, the United States, the international community, including the Russians, will then put pressure on the regime and the opposition to come to a final deal.

The CHAIRMAN. Well, let me just say that in the midst of a civil war having a disparate group of opposition define a national agenda needs a lot of assistance at the end of the day to achieve it. And it also needs to have some understanding of what our baselines for the Russians if we are going to achieve it and see if they can be commensurate at the end of the day.

When I talk about a strategy, this is—I would like to hear—and I am going to move on to Senator Corker. But I would like to hear in some setting the detail of what our effort is, because I just do not get the sense that we are headed anywhere there.

Just one final question. Mr. Countryman, I applaud the work that is being done on the chemical weapons and it is a major concern. But originally public reports had that we knew that there were 45 sites. As I understand it, the Syrians declared 23 sites. So what is the story with what we believe are the rest of the sites, and how are we ensuring that we are getting access to the entire inventory of what we believe exists in Syria?

Mr. COUNTRYMAN. Thank you, Mr. Chairman. On your earlier comment, I just want to say that, while al-Assad may see himself as indispensable to the elimination of chemical weapons, that is not our view. The Syrian Arab Republic, has accepted an obligation that is binding upon this government and binding upon the next government, which we hope to see soon. That is what increases the urgency of both destroying and removing chemicals as rapidly as possible, so that the regime cannot cling to its fantasy that it is an essential part of the process.

We do have a strategy to move forward on chemical weapons destruction. We have a great advantage in this task over all the other tasks in Syria in that there is no opposition to it. Russia, the regime itself, the opposition, the United States, and the world all want to see these chemicals removed and destroyed rapidly. It is therefore not a political issue. It is not an issue on which there is a disagreement between the United States and Russia. It is rather a logistical and a technical issue.

I would be happy to come back at any time and brief on the details of how we will get to complete elimination by the middle of next year.

On your specific question, we have long tracked the sites that we believe are associated with research, development, production, and storage of Syria's chemical weapons program. The number of sites, as you note, that we have tracked is more than 40. The OPCW has talked this week both about visiting 21 of 23 sites and it has also talked about visiting 37 out of 41 facilities. It is not just a semantic issue whether we are talking about sites and facilities, whether we are doublecounting. It is, as you note, a serious question that needs to be addressed.

We received, only on Monday, Syria's 700-page inventory of its holdings. We are studying it carefully. It is a classified document that we would be prepared at a later point to brief in a classified setting. But we do have the tools under the OPCW and under the U.N. Security Council resolution to resolve any discrepancies between what we believe and what the Syrians have declared.

The CHAIRMAN. We will look forward to having a classified session to get to the bottom of how many of the sites that we believe are going to be pursued and what needs to be done to achieve that.

Senator Corker.

Senator CORKER. Thank you, Mr. Chairman, again for your opening statement. I appreciated it.

Mr. Ford, you are a figure that is held up by many in Syria and I want to thank you for coming before us today because you have to be incredibly embarrassed at where we are, and coming in and testifying, knowing what you know is happening in Syria to many of the people that you know. I know it has to be tough for you to do today.

Let me just ask you this. The opposition that you know personally in many cases, are they faring better today since we moved toward trying to destroy the chemical weapons that are on the ground? Are they faring better since we decided not to go ahead with military force than they were before this discussion began?

Ambassador FORD. They are deeply disappointed, Senator, that we chose not to use military force. I have heard just anguish from people that I have talked to over there. And I have had to explain the administration's rationale, and I have had to emphasize to them that our primary goal here is to find a political solution——

Senator CORKER. Let me. I am not so concerned about the military force component. What I am concerned about is I would just like for you to tell me that since we have gone through this pursuit with Russia relative to Mr. Countryman's work, which I appreciate, is the opposition on the ground faring better or worse since we are now pursuing the destruction of chemical weaponry?

Ambassador FORD. Their position on the ground, Senator—I am going to leave aside the morale, which I just addressed. The position on the ground has not changed very much. The regime has made some gains in the north, to the southeast of Aleppo. The opposition has made some gains in the south around Daraa. But as

I said before, neither side in this awful, grinding civil war is able to do a knockout punch right now.

One problem which is really hampering the opposition, Senator, is the really bitter divisions among the armed groups. Even in the last months, al-Qaeda groups, especially a group called the Islamic State for Iraq and the Levant, actually started fighting with the people that we support that were fighting the regime. So Salim Idriss and his people have been fighting a two-front war, which has seriously hampered their efforts against the regime. So in that sense, Senator, I think that in particular has made their position more difficult.

Senator CORKER. Well, and I think the humanitarian situation, as Ms. Lindborg has laid out, is worse than it was a few months ago.

Let me just talk. Look, you know these folks. Some of us have become familiar with these folks in refugee camps after multiple trips. We had a strategy that we were building toward in September—early September. The administration has been incredibly, incredibly slow, and obviously this covert policy that everybody in the world knows about, where we are going to train folks covertly, so we do not have to talk about it in committee settings like this—but basically we have trained about a thousand folks, and our intelligence folks, I guess, can train 50 to 100 a month.

And we had some kind of strategy that was a minor strategy, but basically do we really have a strategy at all relative to the opposition and building their strength against al-Qaeda on the ground and the regime?

Ambassador FORD. Senator, we do. Today, for example, we delivered trucks to Salim Idriss's people inside Syria. That is the first time we have delivered trucks.

Senator CORKER. You were going to deliver those trucks when I was there in August, the next week. Just unbelievable. So you delivered trucks, but does he have weaponry?

Ambassador FORD. Yes.

Senator CORKER. Does he have that lethal weaponry? Oh, he does?

Ambassador FORD. He does have lethal weaponry, Senator. I am not here going to talk about anything except what the State Department is doing. But the logistical help that——

Senator CORKER. The State Department is delivering weaponry?

Ambassador FORD. Senator, I did not say the State Department was delivering weaponry. I said we delivered trucks today. And that is important, Senator, because he has got to have a logistical capability. He was renting trucks before, Senator. So this——

Senator CORKER. I met with Idriss in August and sat down with him, and those trucks were coming the next week. So now you delivered trucks at the end of October.

Ambassador FORD. Senator——

Senator CORKER. Are you satisfied with the strategy we have in Syria right now with the opposition? Do you feel good about it? When you talk to people on the ground and in these refugee camps, do you feel good about the strategy that we have now with these people that we have left out on a limb and told them we were going to support their efforts against this regime and against al-Qaeda?

Do you feel good about what our country is doing with the opposition right now, to allow them to have some kind of say-so in the future of this country?

Ambassador FORD. Senator, there is not a person on my team at the State Department who does not feel frustrated—frustrated by the Syrian problem in general. But I have to say we do provide support to help them against the regime. We provide a lot of support. You may discount what we do, but it matters to Salim Idriss. Every time I talk to him he thanks us for what we do.

Would they like more? Of course they would. They would like more from a lot of countries.

In addition, the work that we are doing to help activists and political people that are trying to hold things together in places like Aleppo and Idlib and Raqqah just to keep the hospitals running, to keep electricity in hospitals, to provide clean water, it matters hugely to them.

Are there greater needs? Of course there are. But our resources ourselves are not unlimited. So we are doing what we can with what we have.

But the problem itself is tragic. I know people myself who have been killed. It is tragic and we want to help them. But ultimately, Senator, Syrians must fix this problem. Ultimately, Senator, it is going to require them to sit down at a table. The sooner they start, the better. But in the meantime, we will keep helping the opposition, Senator.

Senator CORKER. I think our help to the opposition has been an embarrassment, and I find it appalling that you would sit here and act as if we are doing the things we said we would do 3 months ago, 6 months ago, 9 months ago. The London 11 has to look at us as one of the most feckless nations they have ever dealt with.

For you to say that these trucks are being delivered today is laughable. I mean, these things have been committed months ago. I have just got to tell you, I respect your care for Syria, I really do. I could not be more embarrassed at the way our Nation has let people, civilians, down on the ground in the way that we have.

I know that Russia is driving this now. I mean, what we have really done is turn the future of Syria over to Russia. They have their hands on the steering wheel. I do not know how you could feel good about the humanitarian crisis that is taking place. I do not know how you could feel good about how our partners, their feelings about our reliability.

But I want to tell you again, I appreciate your concern for the people of Syria. I cannot imagine you can sit here with a straight face and feel good about what we have done. I hope at some point this administration will sit down and develop a strategy, not only for Syria, but for the region, because it appears to me after multiple, multiple trips, this administration acts on an ad hoc basis, looks for opportunities to slip the noose, as they most recently did in Syria. I hope that you will help them develop a longer term strategy.

The CHAIRMAN. Senator Cardin.

Senator CARDIN. Well, let me thank all three of our witnesses. Ambassador Ford, thank you for your service, a distinguished career in diplomatic service, and all three of you for what you have done.

There are two related issues here. We have a civil war, in which the United States has picked a side. I would agree with the chairman and the ranking member, it has not been clear as to what our role is in regards to that civil war, although we have picked a side and we are providing help to the opposition.

Then there was the use of weapons of mass destruction—chemical weapons. President Obama was very clear that we would not tolerate that, and if necessary we would use force. This committee supported the President in that decision that chemical weapons cannot be used without a response from the international community.

So you are here today to say that you are following up on destroying those or removing those chemical weapons. But I did not hear any one of you say anything about the person who is responsible being held accountable. I hear you say that they are going to be negotiating between the government and the opposition on a new government. I heard you say that Assad will probably not be part of that because the opposition has a veto right. It seems to me that we are so quiet about holding those responsible accountable for international criminal actions and that we seem to be timid in raising that subject because we are afraid that makes negotiations more complicated.

But if you do not mention them, then we are not going to get that type of accountability and people will know internationally it is OK to use these weapons. Maybe they will try to take them away from us, but we can survive. And they should not get that message.

So can you reassure this committee and the American public that our commitment is to make sure that President Assad is held accountable and those responsible for killing the people with the use of chemical weapons will be—part of our negotiating strategy is to make sure that they are held accountable for their criminal actions?

Ambassador FORD. Senator, we have repeatedly stated, repeatedly, that regime officials are going to be held accountable. The State Department's public statement in the wake of the August 21 use of chemical weapons in the suburbs of Damascus specifically highlighted that. And many times I personally, and the Secretary himself, have talked about accountability.

Just a couple of things on that. Number one, with the support of the Congress we are actually training Syrian investigators in how to investigate and develop war crimes dossiers. We are doing that now.

Second, we are in discussions—colleagues at the State Department—with international both governments, organizations, and jurists, about what would be the best judicial structure in which to try these war crime dossiers that would be developed.

We take accountability extremely seriously and we do intend to help Syrians hold people accountable, with the work of international partners.

Senator CARDIN. Will this be a subject on the negotiations between the opposition and government?

Ambassador FORD. I have no doubt of that, Senator, because the opposition will insist upon it.

Senator CARDIN. Will the United States insist upon it?

Ambassador FORD. Senator, we will absolutely support the opposition putting that forward. The United States, Senator, is not negotiating.

Senator CARDIN. I understand that, but the——

Ambassador FORD. The Syrians will negotiate.

Senator CARDIN [continuing]. United States was prepared to use our military to stop the use of chemical weapons. Are we prepared to use our political might to make sure that those who use chemical weapons are held responsible for their actions?

Ambassador FORD. Senator, absolutely, and I have already talked about the resources we are already deploying to help make that happen.

Senator CARDIN. Let me move to a second subject, and that is this humanitarian disaster that is in Syria. One-third of their population has been displaced. They are up to about 5 million internally displaced, 2 million externally displaced. The challenge of getting the relief into Syria to help the people who have been victimized is challenging.

What support are we receiving from the international community to help deal with the humanitarian crisis during the civil war?

Ms. LINDBORG. There has been a massive mobilization of humanitarian assistance. The United States is by far the lead, but there are substantial contributions, especially from Europe. Kuwait hosted the U.N. appeal conference last January and has itself contributed a little more than $300 million.

Notably, Russia and China have contributed very small amounts, and there is a goal to, especially as we look at the very extraordinary needs that continue to mount, to bring as many people into the financing of this humanitarian effort as possible.

Senator CARDIN. Thank you.

Thank you, Mr. Chairman.

The CHAIRMAN. Thank you, Senator Cardin.

Senator Rubio.

Senator RUBIO. Thank you, Mr. Chairman.

Ambassador Ford, let me begin before I ask my questions: I do not want anything I ask or the tone of the questions or direction to, in any way, not reflect on the admiration I have for your service to our country and, not only that, but what you have shown as the consistent interest in the future of the Syrian people. But as a representative of the administration we have a chance to ask you questions about the strategy.

Let me just begin with something I think I know the answer to. I know how you feel about this. You have referred repeatedly to how the future of Syria belongs to the Syrian people. We agree with that, but you also believe strongly, I think, that what happens in Syria is in our vital national interests.

Ambassador FORD. Senator, just the fact that Syria has the risk of destabilizing the region and becoming a base for terrorists operating against us, absolutely.

Senator RUBIO. Right. So I just want to make that clear, because there has also been debate about why do we even care about what is happening in another country. This is not just another civil war. It has implications in the region.

So here is why I ask you that. In a few moments, in the second panel we are going to hear from Ambassador Frederic Hof, who is going to testify, based on his written testimony, that Syria on its present course is becoming the worst of all conceivable scenarios, a failed state basically that is divided between Assad controlling a portion of the country, the Kurds controlling a portion near the Turkish border, and then a vast area controlled by jihadists that could potentially use it—try to use it as a base of operations to conduct destabilizing operations in Iraq and eventually potentially in Jordan.

Would you disagree with that assessment? Is that not at this point the trajectory that it is headed in?

Ambassador FORD. Senator, I agree with that statement. But I would like to add something. That is why it is important for countries in the region, for the Russians, for the Chinese and the members of the Security Council, the Permanent 5, the United Nations. Everybody has to do more, because right now it is going in the worst direction.

Senator RUBIO. Well, the problem with that—and I do not want to get into a debate about it—I am not sure the Russians all really much care about the destabilizing influence of Syria in the region. They care more—in fact, I think it is in their national interest, at least they view it this way, that this destabilization might be geopolitically advantageous to them.

But here is why I am asking you that. The right goal here would have been to try to empower nonjihadist opposition forces within Syria to do two things: Number one, have the capacity to drive Assad out of power, whether it was negotiated or otherwise, and create a functional state to replace him; and number two, to leave no space within Syria for these foreign fighters, these jihadists, to come in and create the operational space and capacity that they have now created.

That would have been the best strategy moving forward. But in order to do that would have required us to identify who these nonjihadist opposition forces were and then to help empower them, along with our allies in the region, to do so.

So I want to again go back to the testimony that Ambassador Hof is going to offer, because he is going to point to the fact that it took us until December 2012 to finally recognize the Syrian National Coalition as the legitimate representative of the Syrian people. And even after that, two things happened: one, the United States and the United Nations continued to recognize the Assad-led government, a situation that, according to his testimony, and I agree with, had enormously bad humanitarian consequences for the people of Syria; and number two, without an alternate government providing services and reflecting the values, nonsectarianism and citizenship, many Syrians stuck with the devil they know, having been denied an alternative that they can see and evaluate.

Lest we think that this is only limited to Syria, I want to go to the testimony we are going to hear in a moment from Dr. Gelb, who will testify that "Yet another major reason for policy failure is a lack of a coherent, plausible, and workable strategy. This is not just on Syria policy," she goes on to say the following: "Mideast leaders, without exception, say they don't know what the U.S. strategy is towards their country and towards the region. they say it's vague and ever-changing."

So I close by asking you this. You say in your testimony "The conflict in Syria has fostered an environment that fuels the growth of extremism and al-Qaeda-linked groups are working to exploit the situation for their own benefit. There is a real competition now between extremists and moderates in Syria and we need to weigh in on behalf of those who promote freedom and tolerance."

"We need to weigh in on behalf of those who promote freedom and tolerance." And I take it you say that because in the absence of doing that, by not empowering these folks, you are actually de facto empowering the people who do not promote freedom and tolerance.

So here is my question: Why did we not do it sooner? Because in foreign policy doing the right thing is not the only thing. You also have to do the right thing at the right time. Why did it take so long to reach this conclusion? And now we find ourselves in a situation where this thing that you talk about doing, weighing in on behalf of those who promote freedom and liberty and tolerance, it is harder than ever, and it may even be impossible. Why did we not do it sooner?

Ambassador FORD. Senator, the Syrian opposition itself from the beginning was very atomized. That is actually how it survived the regime's repression, because it did not have any clear leaders. It was a bunch of different neighborhoods with neighborhood activists. There was no national leadership. It is very hard to build up something that itself is still very incoherent.

It took a long time for the opposition coalition to come together. You are right, we only recognized it in December 2012. That is true, Senator, but it was only formed in mid-November. We recognized it as the legitimate representative 3 weeks after it was established. So I do not think we delayed too long.

Senator RUBIO. You still recognized Assad.

Ambassador FORD. We have reduced the Syrian Embassy here, Senator, to a visa officer and, frankly, that visa officer is there because a lot of the Syrian Americans here want Syrian passports and he is able to issue them.

If I may continue, though, about the administration's policy with respect to the opposition, it is still a problem in terms of the divisions. They fight each other sometimes with the same vigor that they fight the regime, even politically. It took an enormous amount of lifting from us—and I was there personally in the region— as well as some other members of this group of 11, to get the opposition coalition to bring in Kurds, to bring in representatives of the armed opposition so that they would reflect those people fighting on the ground, and to bring in people from these local councils that I referred to, so that it is not a purely expatriate organization.

They themselves only move forward, Senator, at a Syrian speed. I wish they would go a lot faster.

Now, our assistance, as I said, is not unlimited. Do they need more? Sure. We are trying to help them generate resources from other countries as well. This is—in a sense, Senator, it is a multilateral effort and we have helped organize the countries that provide assistance.

The CHAIRMAN. Senator Shaheen.

Senator SHAHEEN. Thank you, Mr. Chairman.

Thank you all very much, both for your service and for being here today.

Ambassador Ford, there has been a lot of discussion so far about what our strategy is in Syria. You have laid out what you believe that to be. Can you talk about how we are judging whether we are being successful or not and at what point we may determine that the strategy is either successful or not successful and we may need to make a change?

Ambassador FORD. Senator, we think that the destruction of the regime's chemical weapons is a huge success if, in fact, it is carried out fully, and Assistant Secretary Countryman talked to that. That was a core U.S. national security interest. I remember when I came to this committee as the nominee to be Ambassador 3 years ago we talked about those chemical and nuclear weapons. So that is a success.

Can I say that our efforts to create a political solution or to contain the civil war are a success? No. We are still working on that very hard. But the situation itself in the country is still deteriorating. But we do not see a way for this to be solved militarily. In a civil war where communities think it is existential, that if they surrender they will be murdered, we have to build a political set of agreements between communities. Otherwise the fighting goes on indefinitely.

Senator SHAHEEN. To what extent are our efforts with the London 11, as you say, actually having an impact? Are we coordinating closely with the Qataris and the Saudis and others who are interested in what's happening in Syria?

Ambassador FORD. Senator, when I compare it to 14, 15 months ago, it is a lot better. There is better coordination of assistance flows into General Idriss and into the political opposition. That is better. But it is not perfect and there could be better coordination still, frankly.

Senator SHAHEEN. How much assistance, lethal assistance, do we still think is being provided by the Russians?

Ambassador FORD. Senator, I have actually never seen a detailed estimate of the dollar value of it, but I can say this, that it is substantial, that it has increased from a year ago. There are more deliveries. And in some cases they are militarily extremely significant. For example, General Idriss was telling me about how these refurbished Syrian air force jets—and he said they do not have very many, but he said the ones they have, when they are refurbished, make a huge difference.

So I think the Russians would help everyone get to the negotiating table faster if they would stop these deliveries.

Senator SHAHEEN. Are there efforts—I am sure there are efforts under way at the United Nations to try and address this and in bilateral discussions. But is there more that we can be doing? Are there more international partners that we can bring to bear to try and address this? And who are they and what are they?

Ambassador FORD. Senator, there is no real effort at the United Nations that I am aware of.

Senator SHAHEEN. Should there be?

Ambassador FORD. I do not think the Russians are going to pay much attention to recommendations from the United Nations. But I can tell you that we have had—including at the level of the Secretary, we have had a lot of discussions with the Russians about this.

I will, if I can, if I can take the time just to share a quick story. Working with some members of the London 11 countries, we were able to actually turn back a Russian delivery. We convinced an insurance company to withdraw its insurance coverage for the ship delivering it. But that is a rare success, Senator, frankly. It would be great if we could make better progress with the Russians.

Senator SHAHEEN. Mr. Countryman.

Mr. COUNTRYMAN. The Russian deliveries have become more significant, probably more significant than what Iran provides in terms of military assistance. I noted Senator Corker's statement of concern about the Russians having their hand on the steering wheel in Syria. There is something to that, but what is not noticed is that that costs the Russians in credibility with the rest of the Arab world and with the entire region when they give their unswerving support to the Syrian regime.

Senator SHAHEEN. Thank you.

Mr. Chairman, I am over my time, but can I ask one more question?

The CHAIRMAN. Yes.

Senator SHAHEEN. For Ms. Lindborg: You talked about the vaccination challenges as we are looking at a potential polio outbreak in Syria. Can you talk about whether there is more that we should be doing to try and address that before it extends across the Middle East in a way that would have significant implications for health and safety to people throughout the region?

Ms. LINDBORG. There is an actual outbreak with the 10 confirmed cases. The concern, of course, is that, as you have probably seen in the papers, each of those cases represents the possibility of another 2,000 cases.

WHO has already mounted both a campaign to vaccinate inside Syria as well as in the region. So they are driving forward. The key will be to ensure that all parties grant access to those workers who are administering the vaccines.

Senator SHAHEEN. I understand that. I would hope that we are doing everything we can to pressure the Russians, the Iranians, and everybody else in the Middle East to support this effort, because it has implications for everybody.

Ms. LINDBORG. Absolutely. We are calling on all parties to ensure that that campaign can go forward.

Senator SHAHEEN. Thank you.

Ms. LINDBORG. Thanks.

The CHAIRMAN. Senator Johnson has yielded his time to Senator McCain.

Senator MCCAIN. I thank you, Mr. Chairman. I thank the witnesses.

Ambassador Ford, I would just like to point out, in response to the chairman's question about a strategy, you articulated goals. You did not articulate a strategy.

To call the categorizing and removal of chemical weapons a huge success, it may be, but we are now in the Orwellian situation where the Russians are assisting us in our irreplaceable part of the scenario of identifying and removing chemical weapons, while delivering, as you just stated, increasing amounts of conventional weapons. As someone pointed out, a mother watching a child starve to death is very—it is not really comforting that that child has not been killed by a chemical weapon.

Your continued reliance on the Russians I find just such defiance of the history of Russian behavior that it is absolutely remarkable.

You continue to call this a civil war, Ambassador Ford. This is not a civil war any more. This is a regional conflict. It spread to Iraq. We now have al-Qaeda resurgence in Iraq. It is destabilizing Jordan. Iran is all in. Hezbollah has 5,000 troops there. For you to describe this as a, "civil war" is a gross distortion of the facts, which again makes many of us question your fundamental strategy because you do not describe the realities on the ground.

Now, a usual mouthpiece for—excuse me. A usual spokesperson for the Obama administration is Mr. Ignatius. Now, he writes this morning in the Washington Post, and I quote, "The centerpiece of U.S.-Saudi friction is the administration's more restrained approach in Syria. Obama has decided to limit the U.S. commitment there to dismantling chemical weapons in a joint effort with Russia, providing humanitarian relief for refugees, who may experience massive suffering and loss of life this winter, and catalyzing a political process to replace President Bashar Assad. What Obama is not prepared to do is topple Assad militarily. 'We are not seeking to help the opposition win a civil war,' said a White House official. While the United States will continue to provide overt and covert aid to the rebels, the goal is to strengthen their negotiations at an eventual peace conference in Geneva, not ultimate"—"not military victory."

Then he goes on to say: "But let's be honest. This is basically a formula for stalemate in Syria, with continued carnage and al-Qaeda growth there."

Did Mr. Ignatius adequately, correctly describe the Obama administration's strategy?

Ambassador FORD. Senator, we do not think there is a military solution to the conflict in Syria.

I agree with you, by the way, it has a regional aspect.

Senator MCCAIN. Do you believe if Bashar Assad has the military advantage on the ground that there is a solution?

Ambassador FORD. I do not think Bashar al-Assad can win militarily either, Senator. He has tried very hard for 2½ years.

Senator MCCAIN. Does he have the advantage on the ground now? Do you believe he has the advantage on the ground now?

Ambassador FORD. Only in a few places, like up around Aleppo. He has a disadvantage on the ground in the east and in the south and even in places like Idlib.

Senator MCCAIN. His killing remains unchecked, Ambassador Ford. Come on, let us—it seems like that is a satisfactory outcome to you. The fact is that he was about to be toppled a year ago or a little over a year ago. Then Hezbollah came in, then the Russians stepped up their effort, then the Iranian Revolutionary Guard intervened in what you call a, "civil war," and he turned the tide. And he continues to maintain his position of power and slaughtering innocent Syrian civilians.

And you are relying on a Geneva conference, right?

Ambassador FORD. Senator, first of all, I would agree with much of what you said there in terms of the balance shifting against him and the intervention of Hezbollah helping the regime enormously. I think more and more the regime is dependent on foreign manpower because of the manpower shortages I mentioned.

But our goal ultimately is to get Syrian communities that are afraid of each other to somehow come to a political agreement. I cannot emphasize that enough, Senator. Until the Alawi community that is backing Assad feels that it will not be slaughtered, it really does not even matter if Hezbollah is there; they will keep fighting. So that is why I talked about the need, while we support the moderates in the opposition, Senator, for the opposition itself also to put forward political proposals. Now is the time.

Senator MCCAIN. Well, again realities of warfare, Ambassador Ford, are that someone believes that they can stay in power, which obviously Assad can, that they are not ready to negotiate their departure. That is a fundamental principle, and for you to think otherwise obviously is bizarre.

But let me just say again, the reason why the Saudis have divorced themselves from the United States of America is because of what you just articulated to Senator Corker: trucks. That is a great thing, trucks. As shiploads of weapons come in to the Russian port, as planeload after planeload land and providing all kinds of lethal weapons, and we are proud of the fact that we gave them trucks.

I am now at a position, tragically, where I now will have to rely on the Saudis to provide them with the weapons that they need, because it is patently obvious that the United States of America is not going to do so. In the testimony of the witnesses who follow you, we are seeing an endless slaughter, and this is a shameful chapter in American history.

I thank you, Mr. Chairman.

The CHAIRMAN. Senator Coons.

Senator COONS. Thank you, Chairman Menendez, for holding this critically important hearing. And I want to thank our panel of witnesses for addressing the concerns of the committee and the many unanswered questions that remain with regard to U.S. policy and our path forward in Syria.

While I am pleased that we were able to find a way to avert the need for military action last month following this committee's strong approval of an authorization of the use of force, in my view we cannot forget—should not forget that Assad has murdered more than 100,000 of his own people, and this unconscionable violence, as you have testified, continues to this day, not only through the heinous attack using chemical weapons that killed 1,500 innocents earlier this year, but through the ongoing grinding, medieval siege warfare that was described in your testimony.

I am pleased some real progress is being made in the removal of the means of delivering chemical weapons and that we are in the process of exhausting diplomatic alternatives to military force. But I find it frankly jarring at the same time that 6 weeks ago we sat in this same room and approved a strong policy, directed in part by President Obama, of holding Assad accountable for his crimes, while also continuing to stand with the Syrian people, and yet today we do not seem to be making progress on a number of those essential shared commitments.

Let me just start, if I could, Assistant Administrator Lindborg. When I visited Syrian refugees earlier this year in Jordan, they expressed extreme frustration, anger, disappointment about delays in the promised delivery of U.S. assistance and support. In your testimony you have documented some of the ways that we have delivered a significant amount of support all across the country.

Would you just say a little bit more about what has been done to address logjams and ensuring the delivery of assistance to Syrians both within Syria, but also refugees in Jordan and in Turkey, and to help mitigate the hugely destabilizing impact of this regional conflict on those vital American allies?

Ms. LINDBORG. Yes, thank you, Senator. There has been a huge international focus and a lot of work in the United States on looking at how to address this really crippling burden of the refugees in Jordan and Lebanon. One of the challenges is that so many of them are not in camps, but living with families and in host communities, where vital infrastructure is stressed.

So we have moved to shift a lot of our development programs in Jordan, particularly in cooperation with the Government of Jordan, so that there is increased development investment in communities that are having stressed water infrastructure, electrical systems, schools, clinics. We have something called the Complex Crisis Fund that is working in communities in the north in particular to increase access to clean water, both for drinking and for their animals.

This is part of what is happening across the international donor community, and there has been a lot of work done to create what is a comprehensive platform so that the relief and the development sides are working closely together, understanding that this is a severe and protracted crisis, so we need to really think of how to maximize our resources.

In terms of increasing——

Senator COONS. Thank you. If you will forgive me, we have very short time periods.

Ms. LINDBORG. OK.

Senator COONS. I would welcome more detail.

Assistant Secretary Countryman, I just wanted to both thank you for your work and your testimony and mention a high-level concern on my part about increasing coordination between the regime and Hezbollah. This terrorist organization, as you have testified to and others have spoken to, is sort of all in on the ground and is an ongoing threat to Israel and has targeted Americans in the past.

Is there any evidence of a transfer of chemical weapons or advanced weapons to Hezbollah, and what sort of risk do you think we face in that regard as this conflict continues?

Mr. COUNTRYMAN. There is no such credible evidence. It is one of the things that drives United States-Russian cooperation on this particular topic, that the Russians share our concern that the longer these chemicals hang around Syria the greater the risk they could be diverted to extremist groups of any complexion, inside or outside of Syria.

Senator COONS. Thank you.

Ambassador Ford, if I might. One of my great concerns about the path that we have taken is the very deep sense of abandonment by the Syrian opposition and the Syrian people more broadly and my impression—I think this is a quote from your testimony—that they fundamentally do not trust the Assad regime and are concerned that external parties will cut a deal at the opposition's expense.

While I recognize the challenges posed by internal division within the opposition, which you have spoken to at length, how has this frustration and this internal division manifested itself in terms of ongoing radicalization on the ground? What do you see as the trajectory? And how do we provide the vital support on the ground for the opposition, the vetted opposition, in a constructive way that pushes toward negotiations? And how are we dealing with the significant sense of abandonment on the part of the Syrian opposition by our recent actions?

Ambassador FORD. It is really important, Senator, in order to undercut recruitment by groups like al-Qaeda for the Syrians themselves not to feel abandoned. I think that is just vital. So we ourselves on both a political level—for example the communique that we issued last week out of London with the other countries' ministers was actually very well received, and it underlined our support, said that Assad had no role in a transition government. It said that the regime is responsible for the conflict.

Politically, I think they got a good message out of that. Not the first time, but it was needed then because of their disappointment about the not military——

Senator COONS. Ambassador, this is the statement that says, quote, "When a transitional governing body is established, Assad and his associates with blood on their hands will have no role in Syria"?

Ambassador FORD. Correct.

Senator COONS. Can we deliver on that?

Ambassador FORD. We can, Senator, when we do get, one day, to a political negotiation along the lines of the Geneva communique, we can solidly defend the opposition's right to veto whoever and whatever goes in that transition government. And as long as the opposition does not want Assad and they veto him, we will back them up.

The CHAIRMAN. Senator Coons, I am sorry. I am going to have to move forward. Thank you, but I am sure we will have the Ambassador available to you.

Senator Kaine has deferred to Senator Markey. So Senator Markey.

Senator MARKEY. Thank you, Mr. Chairman, very much.

I thank each of you for your service. You have got very tough jobs and I think we all know that. I also think that we have to approach all of this with a lot of humility, given what we have learned after we intervened in Iraq and Libya and Afghanistan, after what we have seen go on in Egypt. So we should just have a little humility in the United States in terms of our ability to control events on the ground in these countries in a way that allows us to basically in eye-watering detail be able to move the pieces around inside of any country. I just hope that we all keep a little bit humble here, given what we have already gone through over the last several years, notwithstanding our concern for the humanitarian crisis and our desire to see Assad be removed.

May I ask you, Mr. Ford, if you could just give us a little bit of an update at the al-Qaeda forces coming from Iraq, on al-Nusra, on some of these other extremist groups, in terms of the movement that they are making, where they are making it, and where that support is coming from, so that we can understand the nature of the threat that we see to the moderates being successful?

Ambassador FORD. First, Senator, I appreciate your understanding about the amount of resources we put in and our ability to control everything. I think that is exactly right. Ultimately this is a Syrian conflict. It is not an American conflict.

With respect to al-Qaeda and al-Nusra, they have been very assiduous to take control of borders, Senator Markey. For example, their control of those borders delayed our aid deliveries into Syria. I know there was some frustration expressed earlier in the hearing about the delays. The delays were because we had to wait until our friends in the opposition recaptured border points so we could get aid back in to them.

They have mainly focused on building up Islamic courts and structures of governance well behind the front lines of the fight against the regime. To my mind, Senator, they are, whether intentionally or not, they are almost acting as allies of the regime. It is a huge problem for our friends in the moderate opposition.

The support comes mostly, Senator, not entirely but mostly, from inside Syria. For example, they have captured oil wells in eastern and northeastern Syria and they sell the oil, so that they in a sense are becoming more and more self-financed, which is a real problem. So now we are going to have to work with our friends such as Turkey and Jordan to shut off oil sales that they're trying to do, literally like tanker trucks.

They also——

Senator MARKEY. Are we working right now to accomplish that goal?

Ambassador FORD. Yes, we have started. We have had to.

Senator MARKEY. Great.

Ambassador FORD. We have had to.

But they also rely on things like extortion. They run rackets in cities they control, such as Deir ez-Zor and Raqqah. That is why they are actually now beginning to generate an anti-al-Qaeda reaction on the Syrian street in some of the places they control, which to my mind is a very positive development.

Senator MARKEY. Now, who funded these groups initially in order for them to have the resources to take over the oil wells or to take over these cities in which they are now terrorizing the more moderate elements of the Syrian people? Who financed them from your perspective? Deal with the external resources that have been supplied in order to accomplish those goals for the most extreme groups?

Ambassador FORD. Early on in the Syrian conflict, Senator, when they did not have control of oil wells and they did not have control of borders, they were absolutely getting financing from outside of Syria, through several private networks that were funneling money from places like the gulf, but even places in Europe. So we have also had to work——

Senator MARKEY. Can you name the countries, please?

Ambassador FORD. If I say "gulf" in an open hearing, Senator, I think that that is enough, and in Europe.

So we have now opened discussions with those countries as well about shutting down those networks.

Senator MARKEY. May I ask as well, the Iranians are still providing massive support to the Syrian Government. So even as we are negotiating with them on their nuclear weapons program, they are simultaneously undermining our efforts to bring a peaceful resolution to the war in Syria.

If I may, Mr. Countryman. In the past week it has been reported that the Iranian Government wants to actually purchase eight new nuclear powerplants. How much would that complicate our ability to ever get a resolution if they ever did build eight new nuclear power plants in Iran?

Mr. COUNTRYMAN. The Iranian Government and the Russian Federation have long been in discussion about an expansion of nuclear power in Iran, Russian technology in Iran. They make announcements about it regularly. I think it is unlikely to proceed very far very fast until Bushehr, which has been on the verge of opening for many years, actually does begin to function.

The negotiation of the 5+1 with Iran is complex enough as it is, but I do not believe that an expansion of nuclear power or an intention to expand that will happen much later really adds to the nature of the negotiation we are in right now.

Senator MARKEY. May I just say that Iran is kind of a big part of this whole puzzle because of Assad, Hezbollah. Hezbollah—there it is sitting there—has a separate agenda that is totally contrary to our national interests. We are very fortunate that our deal with the Shah to sell them six nuclear power plants was not completed before he fell, or else the Ayatollah would have had six nuclear power plants worth of uranium and plutonium in that country. That would have been a disaster for us.

And for us to just let them repeat history, because that has still been their plan, to use the civilian nuclear power plants as the cover for a nuclear weapons program—that we have to deal with it now rather than later. We have to make it as part of a program that says: You do not have an inherent right to these civilian nuclear power plants and we are going to block it, because if we do not we will return to this whole issue in another 20 years when those programs get converted to a nuclear weapons program with the next regime.

So I just say to you, it is very important for us to look down the line here, to understand what the Iranians have as their goal, to create a regional hegemony, and Assad is still part of that, because I do not think that article 4 of the Nonproliferation Treaty is any longer valid in terms of the Iranians and their ability to actually qualify for civilian nuclear programs in the future. I just think it has to be halted, and I am going to work very hard to make sure that those eight nuclear power plants are never constructed and no one who is in alliance with us is ever allowed to transfer those technologies in the future under the guise of an IAEA that cannot sit by, from the history that we have already lived through.

The CHAIRMAN. Senator Kaine.

Senator MARKEY. Thank you, Mr. Chairman.

Senator KAINE. Thank you, Mr. Chairman and to the members who are testifying today. An observation and a couple of questions.

Much comment around the table about our frustration, what is our strategy, the frustration you feel doing this work, the disappointment that members of the opposition felt when we did not undertake military action. So we are all grappling with this sort of frustration and challenge, potential loss of U.S. prestige in the area over this and over other items.

I am really wrestling, Mr. Chair, with sort of at the root of this, having voted for the authorization with many members of this committee—and it is a vote I would willingly cast again tomorrow. I felt like crossing that line of use of chemical weapons against civilians necessitated that strong response. I think the fact that you both led us to that point changed the equation for Syria and Russia and created an opening to have the dialogue about chemical weapons. That is a good. That these weapons are being destroyed is a good. That the sites are being identified, the production being destroyed, is a good.

But we see a whole lot of bad and we are still wrestling with it.

But we do have to grapple with one thing. Even for such an obvious good as punishing a country for using chemical weapons against civilians, the American public was not really into the mission. We were not into the mission. Just as measured by what I was hearing from my constituents, they were telling me: We do not want to do this. We do not want to do this.

If the effort had been described when we met in August as we are doing this, not because of chemical weapons, we are doing it to change a regime away, even from a murderous dictator like Assad, I think the population would have been even more overwhelmingly, the American public, saying we do not want to do this, because there is a fatigue that the American public are feeling now about the limits of our efforts in this part of the world. As Senator Markey mentioned, we have had hubris and now we have to have humility about the effects of our outcomes.

So one of the issues I really think we are kind of grappling with—and I hope as a committee we may have a time when it is less back and forth with the witnesses, but with each other, to really talk about what our public is telling us. And again, even with that public feeling, I would vote for the authorization again tomorrow because I think crossing the line on the use of chemical weapons against civilians has got to have a consequence.

But the notion of being more deeply involved in more aid to a shifting and fragmented opposition, there is a reason we are having a hard time coming up with a strategy and one of the reasons is that our public is telling us that they do not want us to do it. And whether that causes us to lose prestige abroad or not, that is what our public is saying to us.

So we either have to make the case differently, explain the stakes in a different way, or grapple with what it means that our public, after 12 years of war in the general real estate, is now feeling fatigued about it.

Those are big, tough questions. Let me jump to some—and I do not have answers to them; I am really struggling with them here—specific things.

Ambassador Countryman, you were asked a question by the chair about this discrepancy in the sites, and you might have addressed it when I was out of the room briefly, but I wanted to come back to that a little bit. The OPCW—we have intelligence that suggests a number of sites. The OPCW has looked at 21 of 23 and might get to the other 2, but they are in contested areas.

But I am assuming that the intel we have about additional sites that were not on the inventory is material that we share with the OPCW and we are trying to get them as much information as we can, so that they can expand the list of sites to be reviewed. This is the first time I have dealt with an issue about OPCW and inspections.

But talk to me a little bit about what we share with them and then how they follow up on this information we give them about the insufficiency of the inventory.

Mr. COUNTRYMAN. Well, I think that we share information appropriately with the OPCW. It is a cooperative process. There are—well, let me start here, which is to say that we have received only on Monday of this week the comprehensive declaration by Syria of its holdings. It is over 700 pages. It is quite detailed. We are assessing it now, and there will be a point at which we will have some assessment of the gaps in that document, differences between what is declared and what we believe we know, that we could discuss in a more closed session.

On the question of sites, we have the tools to reconcile any gaps, any discrepancies. Part of it I think may have a simple explanation. For example, OPCW in its statement yesterday refers to 23 sites, but it also refers to 41 facilities.

Senator KAINE. Right.

Mr. COUNTRYMAN. And covering differences in definition between "sites" and "facilities" is part of the answer. I do not want to speculate on what the rest of the answer is, only to emphasize we have the tools, the resources, to resolve those differences, and we will.

Senator KAINE. One brief additional, if I may. Does the United States have confidence in the OPCW, in their technical capacity, their independence and objectivity?

Mr. COUNTRYMAN. In their technical capacity and objectivity, absolutely. They have done a remarkable job in a difficult security environment so far and we salute the organization and the inspectors of many different nationalities who have done that job.

Senator KAINE. Great.

Thank you, Mr. Chair.

The CHAIRMAN. Senator Murphy.

Senator MURPHY. Thank you very much, Mr. Chairman.

Thank you all for being here. I am sorry that I have missed a portion of the hearing. I had another one right around the corner.

Just a few brief questions, some of which you may have touched on already. I know, Ambassador Ford, you spent some time already talking about the infighting currently that is happening within the rebel group structure. We had a lot of conversation here during our debate about reauthorization about the influence that the Jabhat al-Nusra and extremist groups had within that coalition, some of which as it turns out had come from people that were partially on the payroll of some of those opposition groups.

But I know you have touched on this a bit, but having just come from a conference in Africa in which we were seeing some pretty unbelievable numbers of foreign fighters coming in from Europe and some pretty fierce competition amongst different rebel groups to recruit those foreign fighters, more now, even more dangerous and more extreme than Jabhat al-Nusra itself, can you talk a little bit about the infighting even now within the extremist groups? Forget the infighting that is happening in very public ways, with large numbers of fighters being killed, between the mainstream opposition forces and the extremist forces, but we now have just growing competition amongst Jabhat al-Nusra and their competitors to bring foreign fighters in.

One of the benefits of it seems to be that we can track it pretty well because they spend so much time trumpeting their success in bringing in foreign fighters on Twitter and other social media outlets that we have a pretty good idea of who is going where. But it certainly suggests that the fractures within the opposition are not just about mainstream versus extremist groups.

Ambassador FORD. Senator, you are absolutely right, there is more—there actually now are two al-Qaeda groups in Syria. There is Jabhat al-Nusra, which we have designed as a foreign terrorist organization affiliated to Al Qaeda in Iraq last year, 11 months ago. Now in the last I would say 7 months, the Islamic State for Iraq and the Levant has appeared as a separate entity, with more foreign fighters than Nusra Front has.

Nusra seems to have more Syrians, but Nusra is connected to al-Qaeda and to al-Qaeda's leadership. But at the same time, there is this competing group, the Islamic State, with direct ties out of Iraq. They are fighting each other in some places in northern Syria and also in the northeastern city of Raqqah. In some places, just to make the battlefield even more complicated, there are tactical alliances between elements of the Free Syrian Army and the Nusra Front against the Islamic State.

In some places, Senator, it becomes even more complicated because you have Kurdish militias fighting along with other Arab secular militias, and it becomes quite a hodge-podge.

I would just point out one thing if I may, Senator. Just in the last month we have started to see some efforts by non-al-Qaeda

groups to begin to try to reunite, recentralize. I do not know where
that is going to go exactly, but it was not there 2 months ago. So
I find it as a phenomenon interesting. In fact, in my next trip out
to the region that is a question I will be looking at in some detail.

Senator MURPHY. There is the desire on behalf of a lot of people
on this committee to have America weigh in with greater force to
try to allow the nonextremist elements to essentially win the fight
within the opposition. How does the fracturing of the extremist
wing of the opposition either help or hinder our efforts or others'
efforts to try to empower the FSA and others to win the battle
within the opposition for who sits at the negotiating table ultimately?

Ambassador FORD. In my last trip out to the region, Senator, I
had a number of meetings with leaders of fighting groups in north
and northwestern Syria, and I can tell you—these were the real
commanders. We met them in Turkey. They were happy to get tactical level help wherever they could get it, and they were very up
front about that. So if they had a Nusra unit fighting down the
street from where they were, but against the same enemy, they
were happy to take that help.

I have to tell you, we in the administration regard this with a
bit of caution because we do not want people that we support to
be in turn in bed with the Nusra Front. So this becomes really a
challenge for us in terms of directing our assistance.

Senator MURPHY. Thank you, Mr. Chairman.

The CHAIRMAN. Thank you.

Let me thank this panel. I know several of us—Senator Coons,
myself, I am sure others—Ambassador Ford, would like to engage
you a little further in another setting, and Secretary Countryman.
We are going to want to pursue some of those questions in a classified setting.

With our thanks to all of you, let me call up Ambassador Hof and
Mr. Gelb to our next panel. As we call them up, let me say that
I want to apologize for my need to go to the Senate floor. I have
a new colleague from New Jersey who is about to be swon in and
I need to be there for that event. But I have read your testimony
and I appreciate your insights, and I have several questions that
I am going to submit for the record that I would love to—and
maybe will call you if you will be so gracious as to give us some
of your time to engage.

I think Senator Corker has also.

Senator CORKER. Mr. Chairman, it is my understanding that
what we may do, we have some outstanding witnesses, is to listen
to their testimony and then adjourn the meeting and ask questions
formally in writing, if that is—is that acceptable? OK.

The CHAIRMAN. So with that, let me ask Senator Kaine, who has
been gracious enough to preside during this period of time.

Senator KAINE [presiding]. Well, thank you to panel two. It is a
gift to us, and I am sorry that there is so much turmoil, but it is
at least a positive to be swearing in a new Senator. That is a good
thing. Sometimes the turmoil is not so positive, and that is why
many members are going.

But the written testimony that you have each submitted is
superb, and so we do welcome Ambassador Hof, who is a senior

fellow at the Rafiq Hariri Center for the Middle East at the Atlantic Council, and Leslie Gelb, who we know so well on this committee, the president emeritus and Board senior fellow at the Council on Foreign Relations.

In that order, I would like you to begin with opening statements, and then we will see how we are in time when you finish those statements to determine whether we might ask questions before some of us need to go to the floor.

Thank you.

STATEMENT OF HON. FREDERIC C. HOF, SENIOR FELLOW, RAFIK HARIRI CENTER FOR THE MIDDLE EAST, ATLANTIC COUNCIL, WASHINGTON, DC

Ambassador HOF. Very good. Senator Kaine, Ranking Member Corker, thank you so much for your invitation. I am delighted that you think I can contribute something to your deliberations on what is truly a problem from hell, this problem of Syria.

You have my full statement, so I will compress things a bit in the interest of time. The first point I would like to make if I may is that the chemical weapons framework agreement recently arrived at and blessed by the United Nations Security Council is most definitely a good thing. We have news this morning that Syria has beaten the deadline for the destruction of its production facilities. Much work obviously lies ahead, but an Assad regime that is deprived of these materials is a good thing for 23 million Syrians and for the entire neighborhood.

And yet, the problem of Syria at its root is not an arms control problem. Chemicals are the tip of a very deep and very deadly iceberg, one that will surely, if left unattended, kill all attempts to create a political path, a negotiated settlement to this problem.

The iceberg itself is a deliberate, systematic policy and practice of the Assad regime to target civilians with artillery, rockets, aircraft, and missiles for murder, mayhem, terror, and flight.

Consider the words of the independent international commission of inquiry reporting to the Human Rights Council right after the atrocities of August 21, and I quote. It is very brief: "Government and pro-government forces have continued to conduct widespread attacks on the civilian population, committing murder, torture, rape, and enforced disappearance as crimes against humanity. They have laid siege to neighborhoods and subjected them to indiscriminate shelling. Government forces have committed gross violations of human rights and the war crimes of torture, hostage-taking, murder, execution without due process, rape, attacking protected objects, and pillage."

Now, this independent international commission did not give a free pass to jihadists supposedly opposing this regime in their own depradations. But the commission clearly, clearly identified this practice of systematically targeting residential neighborhoods as the thing that is driving this unspeakable humanitarian crisis that's not only victimizing Syria, but it's swamping the neighborhood, including some important American allies and friends.

Now, I think the Obama administration understands that the chemical agreement itself, as good as it is, only seeks to saw off the tip, the visible part of this iceberg. This is why our Secretary of

State is scrambling to try to put together a diplomatic process that moves Syria in the direction of political transition from this regime to something that is actually civilized.

On its current course, as we heard from the first panel, Syria is indeed rapidly becoming the Somalia of the Levant. One set of terrorists, the Assad regime, is consolidating itself in western Syria. Other sets of terrorists, some affiliated with al-Qaeda, are implanting themselves in the east. The administration is trying to jump-start a diplomatic process that would preempt this worst of all worlds scenario.

Yet the obstacles are very daunting. The entire purpose of a Geneva conference or, if it develops this way, a series of meetings would be to replace the Assad regime with a transitional governing body that would exercise full executive power in Syria for an agreed period of time. This body, as we heard this morning, would be created by negotiations by the regime and the opposition on the basis of mutual consent.

This means that anyone participating in the exercise of full executive power would have to be accepted by both sides. The regime, however, has made it clear in public statements that the person, the position, the prerogatives of Bashar al-Assad are not up for discussion at Geneva. The Syrian National Coalition, which would lead an opposition delegation, is undecided whether or not to attend.

Mr. Chairman, in the interest of time let me just skip to my bottom line. I would conclude by pleading that we not avert our gaze from the humanitarian catastrophe that is unfolding before us, victimizing millions of Syrians and harming all of their neighbors. Mr. Assad seems to have concluded that he can do anything he likes provided he does it without chemicals. His principal external supporters, Russia and Iran, seem to be not at all disturbed by his military's concentration on civilian populations.

If, as I regrettably suspect, political transition will not be on the table in any meaningful way any time soon, then our diplomatic effort, all of it, it seems to me has to focus on persuading Teheran and Moscow to get their client out of the business of war crimes and crimes against humanity. And if we want there to be a civilized alternative to this axis of codependency, the Assad regime and its jihadist enemies of choice, currently dividing Syria between them, then we will have to be more serious about overseeing the process of who gets what inside Syria from external sources in terms of arms and equipment.

[The prepared statement of Ambassador Hof follows:]

PREPARED STATEMENT OF AMBASSADOR FREDERIC C. HOF

Chairman Menendez, Ranking Member Corker, members of the committee, I am deeply honored by your invitation to testify today on the situation in Syria. It is a situation for which the word "appalling" barely suffices. The crisis in Syria has, for more than 30 months, been destroying a country of 23 million people. It has been destabilizing a neighborhood containing important allies and friends of the United States. It has been raising questions about the ability of the postwar international system to halt or at least mitigate politically inspired mass murder. As Americans we have a special interest in how the United States responds to an example of what Ambassador Samantha Power characterized as "a problem from hell" in her Pulitzer Prize winning work.

What I would like to emphasize at the outset, Mr. Chairman, is the humanitarian catastrophe that has resulted from the March 2011 decision of the Assad regime to choose lethal force as its response to peaceful protest. Government witnesses will provide you the latest numbers of deaths, refugees, internally displaced, and Syrians requiring nutritional, shelter, and health assistance. This grotesque situation will only worsen with the onset of winter. Members of this committee who have visited refugee camps have seen the despair of adults and the terror imprinted in the minds and on the bodies of children. The Independent International Commission of Inquiry on Syria, reporting to the United Nations Human Rights Council, has identified the Assad regime's practice of indiscriminate artillery shelling and aerial bombardment of civilian residential areas as by far the predominant cause of this catastrophe. It is, as the Commission has indicated, a program that features war crimes and crimes against humanity. Bringing this loathsome practice to an end and focusing on civilian protection in Syria should be our top diplomatic priority. Twenty-three million Syrians and all of their neighbors will thank us if we succeed.

We are, Mr. Chairman, at a diplomatic turning point in this crisis. There is no need for me to recite the chain of events that began on August 21, 2013, when the Assad regime employed sarin gas to kill over 1,400 Syrian citizens, including many children. Suffice it to say that the chemical weapons framework agreement reached by the United States and Russia, endorsed by the United Nations Security Council, and now being implemented by United Nations inspectors, is a good thing; good, but far from sufficient.

Taking from the hands of Bashar al-Assad and his criminal associates their toxic tools of trade will be a gift of great value to Syrians and all of their neighbors. Yet the mass murder continues, even as we speak, albeit without chemical munitions. We have addressed the tip of a deadly iceberg. It is the iceberg itself—a regime policy of mass terror—that threatens to sink all attempts to arrest and reverse Syria's slide into Somalia-like failed statehood. What is needed is a bridge from the chemical agreement to something that can address the Syrian crisis directly.

Syria is not, after all, an arms control problem. It is, quite literally, a threat to regional and international peace. As matters now stand an informal partition is taking hold, with the Assad regime consolidating its grip on the western part of the country adjoining Lebanon and the Mediterranean Sea. Kurds are trying to defend themselves in the northeast, and much of eastern Syria is dissolving into chaos, with al-Qaeda affiliates and other jihadists seeking to impose their ideas of governance on unwilling populations. This axis of codependency—the Assad regime and its jihadist enemies of choice—has been lavished with arms and money. Syrian nationalists trying to stand up to both sets of terrorists have not. Left on its present course a dying Syria with a dead economy will be hemorrhaging refugees and exporting terrorism for many years to come.

Since May of this year the Obama administration has sought to resurrect a political transition formula for Syria agreed to by the Permanent Five members of the United Nations Security Council and others in June 2012, under the chairmanship of Kofi Annan. The Final Communiqué of the Action Group on Syria called for negotiations between the Syrian Government and its opponents; negotiations that would produce, on the basis of mutual consent, a transitional governing body to exercise full executive power in Syria for an agreed period of time in accordance with human rights standards. The objective of this transitional governing body would be to set the stage for what two United Nations Security Council resolutions called "a democratic and pluralist" political system for Syria.

The formula for political transition arrived at in Geneva did not mention the name "Assad." It did not mandate, as a precondition, the resignation of the Syrian President or his departure from the country. Yet the mutual consent and full executive power clauses of the agreement made it clear that an ongoing role in Syria's governance for the current President and his circle of enablers would be possible only if the opposition agreed to it. Furthermore, the transitional governing body eventually established would wield full executive power, displacing those elements of the regime and its subservient government not preserved via mutual consent.

The challenge faced by Secretary of State Kerry as he tries to resurrect the Geneva formula for near-term political transition in Syria is multifaceted, daunting, and perhaps a mission impossible.

First, the Assad regime has made it clear that it has no intention to cooperate in its own transition. Indeed, early in his service as Secretary of State, Mr. Kerry identified this as a key problem, noting that steps would have to be taken to change Bashar al-Assad's calculation with respect to the desirability of a negotiated political transition from violent clan rule to something civilized. If Assad's calculation has changed at all over the past few months it has moved in the wrong direction. He has been confident of Iranian and Russia assistance and he now regards himself as an essential party to a long-term contract having to do with the disposal of chemical weapons. His Foreign Minister has made it clear that the person, power, and prerogatives of Bashar al-Assad will not be up for discussion in a "Geneva 2" conference.

Second, Iran and Russia support the Assad regime in its rejection of the Geneva political transition formula. Iran needs the Assad regime for two things: Syria's logistical and political support of Lebanon's Hezbollah, whose missiles and rockets are regarded by Tehran as its first line of defense against Israel; and the willingness of Bashar al-Assad to facilitate Iran's political penetration of the Arab world. Tehran fully understands that neither a transitional governing body nor a freely elected Syrian Government would sustain these policies. It is, therefore, "all in" for the preservation of Mr. Assad. Russia, meanwhile, has taken the position that the Geneva formula simply does not apply to the Syrian President. Instead Geneva, according to Moscow, should produce a national unity government—a Prime Minister and Council of Ministers—to replace the current lineup, leaving Mr. Assad in place at least until the elections scheduled for May 2014. Clearly Moscow wants Assad to stay in power. This is why it moved with alacrity on the chemical weapons front. It realized that the regime's use of toxins was the only thing tempting the President of the United States to bring military force to bear against Russia's sole remaining Arab World partner.

Third, the Syrian opposition—fragmented, fearful, and dysfunctional—is disoriented by the prospect of engaging the regime in Geneva and undecided about whether or not to do so. The term "opposition" itself is not terribly illuminating. Clearly al-Qaeda and other jihadist elements in Syria are not interested in seeing the Assad regime replaced at Geneva by a body representing nonsectarianism, reconstruction, reform, and reconciliation. They need the Assad regime as a foil just as surely as the Assad regime needs them. For the purpose of the discussion today I will be referring mainly to the Syrian National Coalition when I speak of the opposition, even though this reference itself is inadequate, as there is no single organization that can claim to represent all or even most of the millions of Syrians opposing the Assad regime.

Nevertheless, in December 2012 the United States and other national members in the Friends of the Syrian People Group recognized the Syrian National Coalition as the legitimate representative of the Syrian people. The logical next step would have been for the United States and others to have helped prepare the Coalition to establish an alternate government on liberated Syrian territory: one that we, as part of a broad coalition, would have recognized diplomatically, supported economically, and helped to defend. That never happened.

Instead the United States and the United Nations continue to recognize the Assad-led government, a situation that has had enormously bad humanitarian consequences for the people of Syria. And without an alternate government providing services and reflecting the values of nonsectarianism and citizenship, many Syrians who still stick with "the devil they know" have been denied an alternative they can see and evaluate. The recognition accorded last December seems now to be meaningless.

The result is that the Syrian National Coalition remains, in its essence, an exile organization. It has sought to create an interim government deployable to Syria, but the United States has made it clear it will not recognize it. Some 13 jihadist organizations in Syria have announced their nonrecognition of the Coalition itself. Is it any wonder that the Coalition hesitates to grasp the presumed opportunity being offered by Geneva? Is it any wonder that Secretary Kerry and his colleagues in the London 11 core group of the Friends of the Syrian People find it hard to secure the trust of the Coalition?

Consider for a moment what this Coalition—an organization not quite sure of its popularity and legitimacy anywhere in Syria and acutely aware of the failure of the West to support nationalist resistance forces affiliated with it—is being asked to do. It is being invited to attend a Geneva conference while its putative constituents are being pounded night and day by Assad's artillery and air force. It is being offered the opportunity to listen to a mocking sermon delivered by Assad's chief of delegation about the inviolability of Bashar al-Assad's status. What exactly would this troubled Coalition get for attending such a meeting? What it fears getting is its political coup de grace. On top of this Russia and the regime are seeking to pack the opposition's Geneva delegation with house-broken, regime-recognized "opposition" figures.

Secretary Kerry and his London 11 colleagues have tried to reassure the Syrian National Coalition, in an effort to secure its attendance at Geneva. They have said, in a communique issued on October 22, that the opposition delegation would have the Coalition in the lead and as its "heart"; that assistance to the mainstream opposition and its military forces would be stepped up; that the purpose of Geneva is political transition, and that the formula agreed to in June 2012 all but rules out continuation of the Assad regime; and that the regime and the opposition alike should publicly affirm their commitment to complete political transition. This wording implies that a "Geneva 2" conference may not take place absent the requisite commitments.

The Syrian National Coalition will soon decide whether or not to attend Geneva in light of these reassurances. On balance I believe it should. Yet one thing is certain: the Coalition does not trust the United States. Pledges of increased assistance have been made and heard before. Questions about the actual desire of the United States to see Assad step aside have been raised. Obviously the Assad regime and its Russian and Iranian supporters want Geneva to be the death knell for what is left of the mainstream, nonsectarian opposition. The threat posed to the Syrian opposition is real. And yet it must take into account the possibility that Washington and Moscow may prevail upon Special Representative Lakhdar Brahimi to convene the meeting, and it should measure the consequences for the Syrian opposition of not showing up.

If it appears that Geneva 2 is going to take place, the Syrian National Coalition should take advantage of the forum to showcase some real leadership. It should come armed with a list of names to present to Special Representative Brahimi representing its idea of the composition of a transitional governing body. It should make that list public. The names should reflect excellence, experience, integrity, and patriotism: a nonsectarian all-star team that might well include members of previous and even the current Syrian Government, provided they are people who have tried to render honest service in spite of the regime. By taking this step a long-awaited alternative to the Assad regime would, at last, come into focus for 23 million Syrians.

The Syrian National Coalition has its work cut out for it if it is to attend a Geneva conference in late November. It will have to appoint and empower a small, cohesive team to make key decisions quickly to avoid crippling, endless debates. It will have to reach deep inside Syria to include in its delegation men and women who have borne the brunt of hardship and sacrifice from the beginning. Indeed, it should make a special effort to insure that Syrian women and young people play leading roles. Woman have suffered and struggled more than anyone. Geneva 2, if it happens, should be used as an opportunity by the Syrian National Coalition to earn the legitimacy it was symbolically granted by the Friends of the Syrian People.

Syria on its present course is becoming the worst of all conceivable scenarios: a failed state divided between international terrorists; a carcass being devoured by violent criminals. People of decency maintain there is no military solution to Syria's travails, and act accordingly in their devotion to nonviolent diplomacy and dialogue. People of a different sort—starting with the regime itself—see things differently: they are unashamed about seeking a military victory. The latter have a significant advantage over the former: they act on the ground to terrorize and kill and they perceive no credible military threat to anything they do, provided they do it without chemicals.

This is why the London 11 communique implies that Geneva 2 should not happen absent meaningful commitments to Geneva's mission: real political transition. Yet even with such commitments a transitional governing body would not likely be created in a single session, even one that lasts beyond a few days.

Our diplomatic effort, therefore, should focus on the real challenge: ending or significantly mitigating the humanitarian nightmare engulfing Syria and all of its neighbors. This means leaning hard on Russia and Iran to get their Syrian partner to stop the slaughter of innocents. The shelling and bombing of population centers simply must stop. For a few days in August of this year it appeared that the United States might stop it: that we might neutralize the tools of terror that rain down ordnance—some of it chemical, but nearly all of it conventional—on unarmed civilians who are targeted simply because they do not live under regime occupation. Kofi Annan recognized by late 2011 that there could be no progress toward a political settlement unless de-escalatory steps initiated by the regime were taken: hence his six-point plan. The recent communique of the London 11 recited elements of that plan as listed in the June 2012 Geneva Final Communiqué. How can a peace conference produce anything useful in terms of political transition when vulnerable civilian populations are being set upon by packs of wolves? With the prospects for transition so low, the United States should pivot diplomatically in the near-term to protection of Syrian civilians as its number one priority. The objective of ending the Assad regime's artillery, air, missile, and rocket attacks on residential areas should be our top near-term priority whether Geneva 2 takes place or not.

While pressing Moscow and Tehran to put a leash on their client, the United States and its allies simply must get serious about arresting and reversing the marginalization of armed Syrian nationalists willing to follow the lead of the Coalition-affiliated Supreme Military Council. These elements need the means to defend their people against regime attacks—supplemented by Lebanese and Iraqi militiamen organized by Iran—and stand up to jihadists working with the Assad regime to divide Syria.

There are those who argue it is too late to make Syrian nationalist military leaders the magnets for patriotic Syrians willing to resist the regime and al-Qaeda; that the United States long ago missed this opportunity. Whether or not it is really too late cannot be known without trying. The last thing we need is an unintended consequence of inaction; a prophecy of impotence that becomes self-fulfilling.

People of good will can and do disagree on matters of objectives, strategy, and tactics in Syria. What should be beyond dispute, however, is a key finding of the Independent International Commission of Inquiry: "Government and pro-government forces have continued to conduct widespread attacks on the civilian population, committing murder, torture, rape and enforced disappearance as crimes against humanity. They have laid siege to neighborhoods and subjected them to indiscriminate shelling. Government forces have committed gross violations of human rights and the war crimes of torture, hostage-taking, murder, execution without due process, rape, attacking protected objects and pillage." Without overlooking or excusing the depredations of jihadist elements, the Commission spelled out a powerful indictment of the Assad regime. Unless we can succeed in obliging this regime to abandon its crime spree against vulnerable populations, the prospects for a negotiated political settlement, whether at Geneva or any other place, is nil.

Senator KAINE. Thank you, Ambassador Hof.
Mr. Gelb.

STATEMENT OF LESLIE H. GELB, PH.D., PRESIDENT EMERITUS AND BOARD SENIOR FELLOW, COUNCIL ON FOREIGN RELATIONS, WASHINGTON, DC

Dr. GELB. Ranking Chair, Ranking Member, members of the committee, I will do my best to be brief.

The start of any effort to make sense out of what we are doing in Syria is to have a serious Mideast strategy. We do not have it. Just talk to the leaders of the nations in the area and you will see that they are confused and dismayed, and their willingness to help us on Syria, to follow our lead on Syria, will depend in good part about our getting our act together in terms of dealing with Iran, Iraq, Arab-Israeli negotiations. These things all fit together in the real world.

As far as Syria itself is concerned, we do have no strategy. I think all of you touched on that point very well. We started out wanting to get rid of Assad. We did not take any efforts, either militarily or diplomatically, that could get rid of him. We drew redlines and then did not do anything about them, walked away from them.

And now we are in a position where it seems we are just going to let this war drag on, with terrible consequences that Fred Hof describes and you know full well the horrors of it.

What I would like to do is to get you to think about another possibility, one that I think could hold some promise in some shape or form. That is this. I do not think that we can supply enough arms to the good rebels—the Sunni moderate rebels, the secular rebels—for them to prevail. And even if we added to that some kind of American bombing presence, which our military does not want and which would be very costly indeed, and we do not know how effective it would be, even then I do not think there would be a military solution.

The Russians, the Iranians, and others would support the Assad regime all the more, and we would have a stalemate at a more horrific level for the people of the region.

So what I would do is this. I would focus on two things: one, what is the real threat to the United States interests? Focus hard and relentlessly on that issue. The answer is the jihadis, Nusra, al-Qaeda, and the Islamists who are threatening to take over that state or good chunks of it. They are the real enemy to us, to the Russians, who fear these Sunni Nusra, al-Qaeda radicals also, to the Iranians who fear them, to the Iraqi regime, to the Alawites who have run Syria, and to the Sunnis seeking to overthrow them. They all understand that the worst thing that could happen to all of them would be a takeover by the Islamist extremists.

That provides a basis over time for us to cajole, push, both the Alawite regime and our Sunni moderate friends into some sort of operating alliance or cooperation against the jihadis. I think there is a real basis for it.

Now, there would have to be political understandings as well, and I agree with all of you who feel that in the end Assad must go. It is very important. But the Alawites have to be protected, and you are not going to get the cooperation from Iran or from Russia, from any of these other countries, unless you do protect those Alawites.

So focusing on the real threat allows us to focus our military aid and our diplomacy. If we do not try to do something like that, I think the only result is what we are seeing—more fighting, more killing, more horrific suffering for the Syrian people and their neighbors.

Thank you.

[The prepared statement of Dr. Gelb follows:]

PREPARED STATEMENT OF DR. LESLIE H. GELB

It is always an honor to appear before this committee. Yours is the most important forum for public discussion of U.S. foreign policy. And no policy can be sustained and prove effective without a full and serious public airing. It was my treat to work for Senator Jacob Javits in the 1960s when he joined this committee.

Please forgive that I offer this paper in the form of an outline. I just learned I would testify this past weekend. And besides, I presume to think that an outline actually might be easier than an inevitably wordy paper for public servants dodging daily tidal waves.

I have spent more than 50 years in the foreign policy world—as a Senate staffer, the Director of Policy Planning in the Pentagon, an Assistant Secretary of State for Politico-Military Affairs, a senior fellow in various think tanks, a correspondent, editor, and columnist for The New York Times, and as the President of the Council on Foreign Relations. I have made my full share of mistakes in practice and in print. In most cases, the failures were caused by lack of true knowledge of the countries concerned. Far too often in foreign policymaking, nations in question are viewed by policymakers here in Washington as squares on a chess board and not living places with cultures and histories and mysterious decisionmaking systems. We often don't know who and what we're dealing with. We learn about our ignorance at the expense of the American people.

Yet another major reason for policy failure is a lack of a coherent, plausible, and workable strategy; i.e., one that honestly examines what we know and don't know about the situation and parties, one that honestly and hard-headedly appraises U.S. interests and the power that our Nation can actually apply and where, and finally one that establishes achievable objectives, not goals that result from ideology and politics.

Pardon the long windup, but in policymaking, the windup is almost as important as the pitch.

I. We need an overall Mideast strategy, not just a Syria policy.

Mideast leaders, without exception, say they don't know what the U.S. strategy is toward their country and toward the region. They say it's vague and ever-changing. It's not nearly enough for the U.S. to simply say we want to try negotiations on nuclear capability with Iran, press ahead on Palestinian-Israeli peace talks, and mitigate the suffering in Syria. It's totally confusing to start saying that the center-piece of U.S. policy is to promote democracy and then simply say that it is beyond us. Mideast leaders don't understand how the U.S. can cozy up to the Muslim Broth-erhood in Egypt and then deny succor to the true Egyptian civilian democrats installed by the military. Our best Mideast friends can't figure out why we have reduced democracy promotion to the holding of elections, when it's quite clear that in countries long dominated by dictators, only the well-organized radicals are best organized to win elections.

If we want true help in Syria—and we need it—we'll need better policies toward Syria's neighbors first. Others will help us in Syria to the degree that what we are proposing to do there makes sense. They will also care about our policies directly toward them.

II. The starting place for making Syria policy is asking ourselves: "who is the big-gest threat to U.S. interests there?"

The Obama administration started out with the position that President Assad was the most serious threat to us, and that he and his regime had to go. As nasty a dictator as Assad is—and he's plenty nasty—he isn't the biggest threat to the United States. He's a threat to anyone who opposes him from within. But his exter-nal policies, like those of his father, are ones that his neighbors, including Israel, lived with without great difficulty—with the exception of Assad's efforts to go nuclear in some fashion.

The biggest threat to U.S. interests comes clearly from the Muslim extremists—al-Nusra Front, al-Qaeda, and other related groups. They represent clear and present dangers to Turkey, Jordan, Israel, Lebanon, and others. Just ask them. With a safe base in Syria, they would promote terrorism against their neighbors. And they would foster religious extremist rule in every one of those countries, and of course, in Syria itself. If you think Assad has enslaved his people, these terrorists and extremists would enslave all, particularly women. And they would make life intolerable for Christians, Shiites, Alawites, and anyone who doesn't believe exactly what they believe.

III. So, how do we build a U.S. strategy against this Muslim extremist threat? The answer is to get all parties to focus on this common interest against the extremists.

The extremists are a formidable fighting force. Fanatics, especially well-heeled ones, usually are. They've been quite successful in gaining and holding territory—and imposing Shariah law.

Assad's Alawites know that the Sunni jihadists, if they come to power, would kill them. They would be killed because they have ruled over Syrian Sunnis and simply because they are viewed as hated Shiites. And the Sunni rebels, the moderates that the U.S. favors, fear them most as well. The moderates know well that once in power, the extremists would treat moderate and secular Sunnis the same as the enemy Shiites.

This profound fear of al-Nusra Front, al-Qaeda crazies is the potential common bond between the Alawites and the moderate Sunni rebels. Of course, they don't like each other, but they hate the radicals more.

IV. The U.S., then, has to use its policies, arms, and aid to forge this alliance be-tween Alawites and moderate Sunni rebels. Both would focus on fighting the jihadis, not each other. And in that context, the U.S. and its allies would provide and expe-dite the necessary weapons and money to the moderate rebels.

There would be a kind of temporary truce between the Alawites and the moderate rebels as they tried to weaken and destroy their shared threat. As part of this truce, the U.S. and Russia would seek agreement from Assad to step down in the context of Geneva negotiations and after the subduing of the jihadis.

Then, an interim government of Alawites and moderate rebels would focus on the rapid development of democratic institutions—laws, courts, civil society, free press, and the like. Meantime, they would share power and, if done peaceably, would receive outside aid. After several years, elections would be held on the under-standing that the resulting government would promote power-sharing based on a federal system. Each group, as a practical matter, would prevail in its "own" part of the country, and oil and gas revenues would be shared, etc.

V. The execution would not be as easy as portrayed above. But the principles above—the strategy—could serve as practical guidelines. It's virtually impossible to visualize any other reasonable end to this bloodshed or any other way to moderate the potential threats of Muslim extremism to our friends and allies in the region.

Senator KAINE. Thank you, Mr. Gelb.

Let me check with the staff. The vote, I was just going to say, is starting right now. It will likely be a 15-minute vote. Let me just—I want to ask—we will ask a couple of questions and then some of us will depart, and we will leave the record open for questions by committee members until 5 o'clock tomorrow for these valuable witnesses.

The statement that Ambassador Ford made earlier was that at the current time neither side has the ability to deliver a knockout punch against the other. Is that an opinion that—I would like each of your opinions about that statement.

Ambassador HOF. Senator, I think Ambassador Ford was exactly correct. At this point, at this point you do not even have a civil war in the sense of much going on in terms of units firing and maneuvering. This so-called civil war looks nothing like, pardon the expression, Grant marching on Richmond, Senator.

Senator KAINE. A little sensitive where I come from. [Laughter.]

Ambassador HOF. What we are really seeing, the primary aspect of the so-called combat is regime standoff weaponry—artillery, aircraft, rockets, missiles—pounding residential areas that it either cannot take through ground forces or has chosen not to take. So you really do not have much in the way of a fluid situation between units at this point.

Senator KAINE. If the chemical weapons were in existence and could be used, that would be a knockout punch. So at least the removal of the chemical weapons from the equation took a knockout punch away for the Assad regime, correct?

Ambassador HOF. I think, Senator, that the chemicals were an important subset of the terror aspect here. I think we have to keep in mind that chemical weapons, as loathsome as they are, accounted in the end for a tiny, tiny, tiny fraction of the deaths and injuries.

Senator KAINE. Mr. Gelb, the idea you put on the table about an organizing principle in Syria is intriguing. What would that idea—extend that idea to how we should be positioning, if that was our goal, how should we be positioning our efforts with respect to the restart of Syria's Geneva discussions?

Dr. GELB. I do not think there is going to be a serious restart of the Geneva negotiations.

Senator KAINE. So you really assume that this is a strategy that assumes that the Geneva discussions at best will be superficial and kind of window dressing, but not substantive?

Dr. GELB. I do. I think you have got to begin to portray, for both the Sunni moderates we want to support and for the Alawites who we cannot allow to be killed—they would be slaughtered, too—a kind of solution for them, which I think ought to take place along power-sharing lines, a federal system.

Then-Senator Joe Biden and I, some of you will remember, proposed a federal system for Iraq as the only way to prevent eventual slaughter there. You have to let each of these communities basically run their own affairs within a united state. We solved our own problem with just such a federal solution. I think we have to put that forward to them, to explain that that is the only way for them to escape the continuing stalemate and the continuing horror of the war.

Senator KAINE. Let me see if Senator Markey has questions?

Senator MARKEY. If I may, thank you, Mr. Chairman.

If you could expand a little bit more on Iran and Russia and what you would propose that we do in order to extract the kind of actions that you believe are necessary for us to bring Assad to the table?

Dr. GELB. Good to see you, Senator Markey.

Senator MARKEY. Good to see you, sir.

Dr. GELB. I have talked to the Russians and the Iranians about this, and I think they are quite sympathetic to the idea. They have not agreed to it by any means, but it suits their interests, because they want to do something in the end that protects their allies, the Alawites, and they are not foolish. They see down the line that Assad is not going to be able to stay in power and that regime is not going to stay in power, but they want enough protection for them, and that this presents somewhat of an answer for them.

So I think we need to have this overall strategy and go and talk to them with that strategy in mind. You cannot just say: Hey, let us have a Geneva conference. It will not work.

Senator MARKEY. Let me just, if I may, because administration officials did not want to specifically call out Saudi Arabia or other nations, we will just call them Gulf States. But do either of you feel comfortable in talking about those individual states by name in terms of what we should be asking from them in terms of reducing the amount of support which is going in to the more radical groups that are inside?

Dr. GELB. Absolutely.

Senator MARKEY. Could you name the countries and what it is you think our policy should be?

Dr. GELB. Yes. The countries are Saudi Arabia and Qatar mainly, although it comes in from some other places as well. But those are countries who look to us for general protection in the region. And I am not aware that we have really leaned on them about some of this aid to the jihadis, and we should.

Senator MARKEY. Mr. Ambassador.

Ambassador HOF. Senator, I think it is critically important, and I recognize the operational difficulties of this. This is not a silver bullet, it is not a panacea. It would be very, very hard to do. But I think the United States has to insert itself as the overall supervisor of who gets what in terms of external military assistance going in to opposition groups in Syria.

In order for us to do that effectively, my sense is—and I realize there are reservations about this—we have to have some skin in the game. I know that there are departments and agencies of the United States Government that have spent a lot of time identifying elements inside Syria we want to support. I believe that we have from the Saudis and Qataris and others agreement in principle that the Supreme Military Council should be the conduit.

The problem is we need to be out there in charge of what is happening, just to make sure.

Senator MARKEY. Can we be in charge if we are not providing an additional massive increase in lethal weaponry?

Ambassador HOF. I do not think we can, Senator. I think this needs to be a Department of Defense activity. I think we need to scale this up and get serious.

Senator MARKEY. If I may, Mr. Chairman, if I can just take it a step further.

Senator KAINE. And Senator, if I could make this the last question. I do not want you to mess up your 30-plus year-perfect voting record as a Member of Congress.

Senator MARKEY. I cast the 11th largest number of votes out of 10,850 Members of the House since 1789 and so far I am perfect in the Senate. I was not in the House.

If we did dramatically increase our military, what would the response be from the Saudis, from the Iranians, from the Russians, from Qatar and others? Why does that give us a leadership role with them? Why does it not just lead to an escalation rather than a reconciliation?

Ambassador HOF. I think the practical problem we face right now, Senator, is that people who are Syrian nationalists, people who are dedicated to the idea of a nonsectarian government of citizenship in the future, are the ones finding themselves squeezed out of the picture as private money from the gulf plus what Ambassador Ford described as activities inside Syria are funding al-Qaeda-related groups and other jihadists. They are flush with money. They are flush with weapons. The regime, on the other side, is being supplied lavishly by both Russia and Iran. It is the people in the middle, the people who actually stand for the kinds of principles that I think everybody in this room would be comfortable with, who are not getting what they need.

Senator MARKEY. Thank you.

Dr. GELB. Mr. Chairman, could I just have a minute.

Senator KAINE. Mr. Gelb, I am going to let you have the final word and then we will adjourn, please.

Dr. GELB. It will just take a minute. I disagree with my friend Fred Hof on this. I do not think the answer is to put a lot more arms in there, although we should be putting some more arms in there. I think the way we can lead, take care of our interests, is to have a strategy that makes sense to the countries in the area, so that they will go along with it.

They are not going to go along simply because we are providing more arms. It will not work.

Senator KAINE. Thank you both. The record will stay open for additional questions for these witnesses or the first panel until 5 o'clock tomorrow. We appreciate your testimony and thank you for your patience today.

[Whereupon, at 12:17 p.m., the hearing was adjourned.]

ADDITIONAL MATERIAL SUBMITTED FOR THE RECORD

RESPONSES OF ASSISTANT SECRETARIES ROBERT FORD AND THOMAS COUNTRYMAN TO QUESTIONS SUBMITTED BY SENATOR JEFF FLAKE

Question. Throughout the Syrian civil war, the Obama administration has supported a negotiated political settlement to the conflict but has maintained that Bashar Assad must go. However, some experts have suggested that the framework now in place to eliminate chemical weapons in Syria has, in effect, created a U.S. interest to keep Assad in power. Assad himself seems to be emboldened by recent events, having said in a recent press interview, "I don't see any reason why I shouldn't run in the next election."

♦ What is the administration's position on Assad remaining in power? If Assad were no longer in power, what would happen to the framework currently in place to eliminate Syria's chemical weapons program?

Answer. The administration supports a transitional governing body in which Assad and his close associates have no involvement. With regard to the elimination of chemical weapons in Syria, the United States will hold the Syrian Government, whether it is the Assad regime or a successor government, accountable for Syria's obligations under the Chemical Weapons Convention and U.N. Security Council Resolution 2118.

Question. The opposition in Syria remains adamant that Assad not be a part of any future government in Syria and has made that a sticking point in their negotiations. How has the framework to disarm Syria affected the peace process?

Answer. The international community is working to bring the opposition and the Assad regime to the negotiating table to develop a sustainable solution for peace in Syria. The Geneva Framework for the Elimination of Syrian Chemical Weapons shows that the Russians are willing to pressure the Assad regime and that this pressure can help shape their behavior. We believe the regime used CW in part to compensate for a shortage of trusted, battle-capable regime troops. The international effort to eliminate Syria's CW will have a military impact, and we hope that this will provide a foundation for the wider political negotiations at a Geneva II conference.

Question. Recently, the Deputy Prime Minister of Syria—who is not a member of the Baath Party and has been described by the Wall Street Journal as having "joined the government . . . as [a] representative of the so-called internal peaceful opposition as a way for Mr. Assad to show his readiness for some reforms to help end the country's war,"—was fired by Assad while Assad was in Russia. He was apparently fired because he met with you in Geneva to discuss peace negotiations.

♦ In your view, why was Mr. Jamil dismissed? Do you view Mr. Jamil's dismissal as a sign from Assad that he is not sincere about future peace negotiations?

Answer. We cannot speculate on the inner workings or sincerity of the Assad regime. The United States is committed to ensuring that the opposition accepts the Geneva Communiqué. The Russians have indicated that the regime is still open to negotiations and we expect that they will make clear that the purpose of these negotiations is to implement the Geneva Communiqué.

Question. The administration's policy toward the Syrian civil war has gone from taking a hands-off approach and supporting a political settlement, while arming some of the rebel factions, to unenforced redlines on the use of chemical weapons, to requesting authorization of the use of military force to degrade and deter Assad's chemical weapons capability, and now to supporting the elimination of Syria's chemical weapons program.

♦ Ambassador Ford, can you please describe to me what the ultimate goals are for Syria and how the administration plans to achieve them?

Answer. We do not believe there is a military solution to the crisis in Syria and therefore support a genuine political settlement that can bring an end to the bloodshed, preserve state institutions, and prevent the conflict from spilling into neighboring countries. Negotiations are the only means to reach such a settlement; they should not be open-ended and must result in implementation of the Geneva Communiqué principle of a transnational governing body that holds full executive authority.

Question. According to CRS, the United States has provided "$6 million in financial and in-kind assistance to the OPCW and United Nations" for Syrian disarmament.

♦ How much will disarmament cost before the task is completed, and how much of that cost will be borne by the United States? Have any funds designated as "Overseas Contingency Operations" funds been used to achieve this goal, and will any such funds be used in the future?

Answer. The approximately $6 million in financial and in-kind assistance the United States has provided to the OPCW and United Nations was drawn from the Department of State's Nonproliferation and Disarmament Fund.

Specific plans for elimination of Syria's remaining chemical weapons program are being developed by the U.N.–OPCW Joint Mission, and it is premature to discuss specific destruction details or costs until a destruction plan has been finalized, which we expect to occur in mid-November.

○